Remember Me? – Getting Your Home Based Business to Stand Out in an Over Marketed World

Kris Valdez

ISBN:0989067505
ISBN-13: 978-0-9890675-0-8

DEDICATION

This book is dedicated to God, who gave me
the words and patience to bring this work to fruition. My
husband, who is more than I could ever want in a husband
and father. To my kids who are the reason I strive to be
better today than I was yesterday.

CONTENTS

ACKNOWLEDGMENTS

I'd like to acknowledge those who helped make this book a reality. First, I want to thank, Michelle Sugarman with Leading Synergies, for being an amazing life coach and supporting me through this process. Second, to a talented editor, Lauren Ruiz with Pure Text, who did an incredible job shaping this book while keeping my writing voice intact. To Robyn Ritsch of Axis Sports Medicine for getting me walking again and becoming a lifelong friend. To my dear friends, Mara, Charmin and my sister Melissa, thank you for getting me through the tough times. To my parents who always encouraged me to write and my mom for being my first editor whether I liked it or not. Last, but not least, thank you to my family for their understanding and patience while writing this book. Without you, any success wouldn't mean as much.

Thank you all!

INTRODUCTION

Marketing strikes fear in the heart of most home-based business owners. Because they have no idea where to begin, the majority of people would rather visit the dentist for a root canal than start working on their marketing strategy. They could start with placing an advertisement here and there or making the dreaded cold calls or putting themselves out there at a networking event. But while these are all pieces of marketing, none of them encompass marketing. The purpose of marketing is to stand out. The cry of every business is, remember me?

One of the most important parts of marketing is having an overall view of your business. Mapping out a plan for the future of your company is critical for you to be able to get where you want to go. Here, in the first few lines of this book, is the key to marketing: be consistent and persistent. This should become your business marketing mantra. A home-based business owner can have a mediocre marketing plan at best and still succeed if they spend a few minutes every day or even every other day implementing that plan.

The biggest questions most people have after reading the leading marketing books is, "If I don't have an existing business or if my business is too new, how am I supposed to develop a target market? What should my numbers look like? Whom do I network with?" No one can definitively answer these before a business gets started. It is all guesswork, otherwise known as calculated estimation, as well as a little trial and error. Right now there is shock and dismay coming from some of your lips, but yes, marketing involves a lot of educated guesswork.

It is a cold hard truth that even big company products that have months, sometimes even years, of research behind them fail. Anyone remember New Coke? To compete with Pepsi, Coke conducted taste tests to see if people would like a new formula that was closer to Pepsi's. During the taste test, people said they liked the taste of the product and would definitely buy it in stores. When New Coke arrived on store shelves, the results were disastrous, no one was buying and faithful consumers were outraged that their favorite drink had changed." Coke was able to recover by bringing back Coke Classic, but most small businesses could never overcome such a marketing calamity.

Since it is not the intention of this book to have you give up on marketing before you even get started, let's put the mistakes of Coca-Cola aside. Within this book are simple, small, low-cost steps every home-based business owner should take to begin their marketing strategy and in turn put their business on the road to success. The purpose of this book is to provide you with the information needed to stand out in this over-marketed world in which we live.

Remember, the choices you make today impact the future of your business tomorrow. Are you choosing success or failure?

1 DEFINING THE COMPONENTS OF A MARKETING PLAN

It's Monday morning as you stroll into your home office with coffee in hand, smiling down at your bunny slippers, and flip on the snoozing computer. There, in your inbox are all the inquiries about your business that have come in since Friday. You respond to each one and look forward to working with new potential customers. Your calendar in Outlook is booked solid, except for the slots that would conflict with the kids' schedules and your favorite guilty pleasure on television. As you review your week your website is alerting you to new leads in your target market. All this and you haven't even hit the shower yet.

Does this scenario sound too good to be true? This is the reality for some home-based business owners, and it could be your reality too. The difference between your business and the one in the scenario is marketing. People with successful businesses learn the marketing tools that work for them as well as their target market. Then they implement those tools on a consistent and persistent basis.

Getting Serious

Many home-based business owners claim they do not have time for marketing because as home-based business owners, they are the chief executive officers, chief financial officers, chief information officers, and chief janitors. If your business is not marketed on a daily basis, though, all the other positions will not matter because they will not exist.

The biggest mistake home-based business owners make is flying by the seat of their pants. It is similar to taking a road trip to an unknown destination without a map. Granted there might be a GPS system to show the way, but it'll be useless if you don't know where you are going. Will there be short-term goals (any rest stops?), long-term goals (will you stay for the weekend?), or a combination of both? What is the starting point?

As a home-based business owner, you must treat your company like a serious business. While that may sound elementary, think about how you spend your day at the office. Do you take personal calls during your business hours? Do you take time off to play a round of golf, do the laundry, think about your grocery list, or plan what you're having for dinner? You don't have to be stuck at your desk from 9 a.m. to 5 p.m. and schedule marketing between 1 p.m. and 2 p.m. (unless of course you like a ton of structure in your life). But working from home is not a green light to goof off. Take marketing your business seriously, and your clients will take you seriously.

What Is Marketing?

Defining marketing is simple: marketing is bringing your products or services together with the people who need and want them. The hard part is letting those people know about your products or services. Even if the time is made to market a business, if it is not marketed correctly, its owner may end up doing more harm than good. This is where marketing tools in conjunction with a defined marketing strategy come into play.

The most important thing when defining and developing a marketing strategy is getting it on paper. When small business owners say their marketing plans are all laid out in their heads this is a giant red flag. Even if your marketing strategy is only one page long with bullet points, by having it down you are already way ahead of those who have it all worked out inside their heads. From now on, put everything in writing. But don't let it sit collecting dust on an office shelf; make sure to review your marketing strategy and adjust it regularly.

Make Marketing Personal

Before learning the components of a marketing plan, you need to know about the personal aspects of marketing that are rarely addressed in marketing books: people want to market their businesses, but fail to by falling into three different categories of marketing ruts.

Where Do I Start?

The first is not knowing where to start. For those of you in this crowd, this book will help you define goals, identify your target market, choose marketing tools, and implement your chosen strategy. While there are many marketing options laid out in the coming chapters, do not feel overwhelmed by the number of marketing avenues available to you. Choose which ones work best for you and your business. Later, when your business has grown, try the other marketing tools that interest you.

Excuses, Excuses

Then there are some who have the know-how, but create hundreds of excuses to do something else at home. To people who fall into this rut, doing the laundry or maybe cleaning the dust bunnies out from behind the refrigerator sounds more appealing than implementing a marketing strategy. It is easy to get distracted, especially as a home-based business owner. This book will help you focus your marketing efforts and rework the strategy you already have or help you develop one you can be excited about.

Where Are the Results?

The final rut home-based business owners fall into is working their existing marketing strategies that were possibly even put together by professionals but not yielding the results that were hoped for or promised. This book will jump-start your creative juices and help you take a fresh look at the way you are marketing your business.

First Steps

By having this book, you have taken the first step to having a successful home-based business. Congratulations! The next step is to use the tools and practices that it outlines. Not all the suggestions will be right for your business however. This book provides an overview of many different options that can work for your home-based business, but it is up to you to choose which will work best for you.

For example, later, we will discuss some rules for networking effectively, but if you are scared to death of a meet and greet, then this won't be the best option to showcase your company's products or services. The same goes for giving a seminar or speech to a group in your target market. Even though the setting may be perfect, if you shake, sweat, and stammer during your presentation, the opportunity will do more harm than good for your business.

First Questions

Before you can begin working on your marketing strategy, you must ask yourself these questions and think about them as you read through the book. Then come back and answer them before putting your marketing into action.

What environment am I most comfortable in?

How do I interact with people?

What can I teach people about my products or services?

How do I want to present that information?

By answering these questions and knowing what makes you tick, you can choose the marketing tools that best fit your personality. Marketing your company is as much about the products or services as it is about you. You probably don't have sales people to manage, so your home-based business is a reflection of you and using marketing strategies you love will translate into more satisfied customers.

One Final Question Before We Start

The final question to ask yourself is, "Am I operating my business from a place of fear or from a place of prosperity?" In other words, are you trying to keep your business from failing or are you trying to make it successful? There is a big difference between these. One is scraping from the bottom of the barrel and hoping that the next cold call, advertisement, or networking event will bring in the home run deal. The other works within, or just outside, your comfort level, and comes from your belief that your company enhances others' lives, making you excited about offering them the opportunity to work with you. Having the latter attitude presents an image of assistance rather than of desperation.

It is important to know where you're coming from because thoughts and words, even unspoken, have power over our lives. If you desperately need or want the next sale, it will show in your business approach. People can feel desperation. If you see yourself as already successful and the next sale is icing on the cake, then that will also show in your business approach. Success is how you define it for your business. It could be making five sales calls in one day or booking a presentation, it's up to you to define, but build your business from a place of triumph.

Give the prosperity question some thought and work through it. Maybe even jot down your answers on a piece of paper or type them out. The way you answer this question will determine how to best market your home-based business and how to make your marketing work best with your personality.

The Critics

When you tell people that you are thinking about starting, or have started, a home-based business, no matter what industry it is in, you get two types of reactions. The first is excitement, and the extending of congratulations. These people may even want to know how they can help you along in your new adventure. Remember this group and keep their phone numbers handy when you begin your marketing strategy.

The second reaction is criticizing and balloon popping. These people want to dash your dreams of owning a successful home-based business. Their reasons could stem from jealousy that you are brave enough to give it a try. Whatever their reasons, though, listen to the objections of this group openly. Figure out where their criticism is coming from and whether it is reasonable. Perhaps your home-based business is offering the right products or services, but at the wrong time. Sometimes outsiders can see things more clearly than we can. Though they may be concerned for your well-being, it is up to you whether or not you want to take their criticism to heart.

However, if you have thoroughly researched your business idea and know there is a market for it, do not let the naysayers make you scared to proceed with your home-based business. Make the decision right now that your business will succeed. Leave no other options. Even say out loud that your home-based business is successful. Let no one stop you from pursuing your dreams of excellence.

The Rest of the Story

By now, you may have noticed that you will not be developing a full-blown marketing plan. That would involve large amounts of data, forecast models, and independent research as well as a lot of time and money. Developing such an extensive marketing plan is an unnecessary expense for a home-based business owner anyway. Rather than spending your efforts predicting behavioral patterns that sometimes even the big companies get wrong, you will be implementing immediate and practical strategies for success. The rest of this chapter briefly covers what this entails.

The Mission Statement

While the mission statement is what encompasses the identity of your business and is one of the first things read in a marketing plan, most marketing books state it should be written last. But with this book you will not be creating a typical marketing plan.

The mission statement is the vision for your company to work towards, so before you go any further develop a short mission statement. Go on, write it. The rest of the book will still be here when you are done. To get yourself started, close your eyes and envision where you want your home business to be in one year, two years, and five years. Pick one central idea from that image. An example of a central idea is be the utmost authority on home-based business marketing and encourage women to follow their dreams to completion. Now write your marketing mission statement around that idea.

The mission statement should be simple and straightforward. It's made up of a few sentences that tell potential customers about your home-based business and what motivates you to serve them. This is just a starting point: your initial stab at your mission statement is not set in stone.

Refining the mission statement should be easy once your marketing strategy is done. If you have employees or contract help, make sure each person working for your company memorizes the mission statement. Everyone who represents the company should believe in its mission. The people representing your business are walking and talking billboards for your products or services and should encompass your mission statement. Make sure you and your employees are projecting the correct image about your business.

Examples of Mission Statements

The mission of Novel Ideas is to assist and encourage other women business owners with their marketing objectives through coaching and freelance writing.

Warm Hands Massage Therapy is dedicated to creating long-term client relationships by being professional but fun while offering flexible business hours through in-home services.

Goals and Objectives

Another element of the marketing strategy is defining the goals and objectives for your home-based business. There must be a perfectly clear message to focus your clients on the specific products or services you offer. Without clearly defined goals and objectives the business will not have any way of measuring success. Not only will spelling out your goals and objectives make it easier to track your success, but it will keep you motivated on tough days. Developing your goals and objectives will be covered in Chapter Two.

Description of Your Products or Services

Are you able to summarize what you offer to potential customers in less than 10 seconds? Are you able to expand on that original description, providing additional benefits, in less than 30 seconds? This is where you define the Unique Selling Position (USP) of your products or services. Discover the differences between your company and another, and then build on those differences. Determining your USP will be covered in Chapter Three.

Defining Your Target Market and Your Customer Profile

As stated in the introduction, there is no magic bullet in marketing, but there is a way to make better use of your marketing money: defining your target market and developing an ideal customer profile. If you have these things in mind when you are using your marketing tools, the better your return on your marketing budget will be. The specific steps to do this will be covered in Chapter Four.

Know the Competition

In this age of the ever expanding Internet with its online databases, government reports, statistical data, and endless websites, there is no excuse not to get the dirt on your competition. A word of caution however: do not get so sucked into researching other companies that you get anxious about marketing your own. Do not worry about their spinning logos or about the flash presentation on the opening page of their websites because that might not be what your ideal client wants to see anyway. Never be intimidated by your competition. Just get to know them and then exploit their weaknesses within your target market and ideal client base. Chapter Five covers how to study the competition on a small budget.

Image and Design

This is the fun part for many home-based business owners because they see it as their creative outlet. While there are numerous computer programs that allow you to design your own collateral material, if you can afford it, this is where you should spend your money. Unless your home-based business is a graphic design company, developing your image should be done with some help, even if it is just from one professional whom you can use as a sounding board. The information in Chapter Six will cover what you should incorporate into your collateral material and how to use your image to help sell your products or services without you even being there.

Marketing Tools

This is where the rubber meets the road, so to speak.

Using just one of these tools will not make your home-based business a success, but using different marketing tools in conjunction with one another will have your business heading on an upward trajectory to success. Chapter Seven covers the ins and outs of networking, Internet marketing, referral building, promotional events, and media outreach. This is where you will choose the tools that fit best with your personality and business.

Implementing the Marketing Strategy and Building Relationships

By this point, you will have put pen to paper or keyboard to computer screen and written out your mission statement, your goals and objectives, and the description of your products or services. You will have defined your target market, researched your competition, figured out your image, and chosen your marketing tools. The next step will be the implementation of your marketing strategy and finding clients.

Building a relationship with your client is similar to the dating process, minus the roses, the candy, and the breath freshener (okay, maybe it does include the breath freshener). Sometimes one of the most difficult parts of having a client base is keeping clients happy. Chapter Eight covers how to maintain a balanced and healthy relationship with your clients while implementing your marketing strategy. Boundaries anyone?

Marketing Reviews

This is the chapter that brings it all together, where you learn to find out what has given you the best bang for your buck. For the sake of your bottom line, this is the step that counts because it shows you what worked and what did not. Chapter Nine gives you ideas on how to make marketing your home-based business a daily practice and how to learn from successes as well as mistakes.

Final Thoughts

Marketing your home-based business is a marathon, not a sprint. Take time to understand the principles, practices, and strategies in this book, and you will see positive changes in your business. Your successful marketing journey begins now.

2 IDENTIFYING THE BUSINESS WITH GOALS AND OBJECTIVES

At this point, you are not figuring out your logo, your webpage layout, or even your business card design. Before you can discover your image, you must identify your business. This sounds simple but people overlook this step, especially in home-based businesses, because they might only look at a company, products, or services that could make them the most money. But having a successful home-based business means combining your passion with a marketable niche. In order to do that, you have to ask and answer questions to figure out what makes your business unique.

The first question you need to ask yourself is, "What do I want my company to look like?" Actually close your eyes and imagine the best possible scenario for your company. Ask yourself the following questions:

Why did I start this company?

What do I want to accomplish with this business?

What is my company offering?

How is it different than any other business?

What do I want my potential customers to know about me and/or my company?

What image do I want to present to potential clients?

Do I want people to know that I am home-based or should I develop a virtual office space?

How do I want this business to end? Use this question to determine whether you want your business to end with you or whether you want to model your marketing so your business can be sold or passed on to your children.

Developing business objectives goes beyond defining your products or services. Be crystal clear on what your company is and is not, because if you don't know what your company stands for, no one else will either. Find the one thing your company does well and focus on it like a laser beam.

Write down the ultimate vision for your home-based business. Define specific overall objectives that you wish to incorporate into your business by answering and expanding on the questions listed above. Once you know what your ideal business will look like, take steps to get it there.

Defining Your Market Position

There are different directions in which you can take your
company image. The one you choose will determine the
value your clients put on your products or services. What
do you want your perceived value to be? Do you want to
be number one in the market, the most respected, or the
producer of the highest quality? As an exercise, imagine
your home-based business as the Yugo, the Volvo, and the
Bentley of your niche.

The Yugo

As the Yugo, your business will be the lowest priced
option in your market. It might take some work on your
part to make sure you are indeed the lowest priced. Not
only will you have to work hard to guarantee another
business owner doesn't underbid you, but the volume of
work needed to cover costs while working at a lower rate
may run you as well as your business into the ground.
Before marketing your business based purely on price,
make sure you are up for the work it entails.

Because your products or services do not have all the bells
and whistles of the higher priced competitor, you will have
to answer the question of why customers should choose
the lower priced option rather than getting better services
or nicer products. Right now you may be saying, "Wait a
minute, I am going to offer just as much as the expensive
guys but at a lower price. Since I am a small business, my
customers will receive personal care." Think about that,
though. There is no way you can sell on price and still
offer the same service and added benefits as the more
expensive alternatives without seeing a little profit for all

your hard work. The main point of your home-based business is to make money. If you are pricing yourself as the least expensive alternative, make sure that your budget will be in the black rather than sliding into the red.

The Volvo

While this car is seen as classy, its notable feature is safety. Your business can be the safe and reliable option for your clients. Not only can safety be communicated through color choices and design, as will be discussed in Chapter Six, but offering a guarantee for the products or services you are providing will alleviate most buyers' minds before they part with their money.

The Bentley

As the Bentley, you will be the best of best, the most exclusive, and the most expensive, but you'll be worth every penny because of the products or services your clients will receive. This strategy will mean fewer clients, but a higher return on your efforts.

The key to being seen as the Bentley of your market is having everything you offer exude class, prestige, and exclusivity. This means investing more time and money cultivating your prospects. It may be difficult as a home-based business to front the money needed to be in this market position, but if this is where you strive to be, do not nickel and dime your way to the top: Spend the money up front to position yourself as worthy of the price you are asking. Then have the materials, reputation, and knowledge to back it up.

Be a Laser Beam

The surest way to failure is diluting your message. Trying to be all things to all people will never work because customers or clients won't know how to categorize you. This means: don't have your marketing materials scream Yugo as you charge Bentley prices. For clients to know how to classify you, your image needs to match your collateral. People like to know who to call when they have a specific need. If you are a jack-of-all trades and a master of none, they won't call because your business will not be seen as the best answer for problem x, y, or z, but as an only okay answer to all.

S.W.O.T. Team

To fully define your business, keep asking yourself questions. Defining your business is an extensive thought process, but it needs to be done. Once again, put pen to paper or keyboard to computer and answer the S.W.O.T. questions.

No, this doesn't involve putting together a team of people in full riot gear with guns blazing—unless of course your business is personal security for a head of state. Oh, wait, that's S.W.A.T. (although it might not be a bad idea to envision your marketing plan as a skilled attack on the competition). S.W.O.T., though, stands for strengths, weaknesses, opportunities, and threats.

The Strengths

The strengths of your company come from the skills, abilities, resources, and competitive advantage your team brings to the table. Even if your home-based business is a party of one, you have special talents that only you bring to the table. Every company is different and it might take a little digging, but you can stand out from your competition with your unique strengths. So pull out your sand shovel and begin to unearth your strong points.

The Weaknesses

The second letter in S.W.O.T. stands for weaknesses. It is not much fun to look at our weaknesses, but doing so is necessary to understand where help or improvement is needed. Examine the negative qualities of your company and what skills are lacking that give the competition the upper hand. If you have trouble identifying your weaknesses, ask someone else to. A best friend, the person you're dating, and your mom, unless they're one of those critical types, are probably not the best candidates for this job. Find a person whose opinion you trust and value to be honest about your blind spots.

The Opportunities

More fun to consider are the opportunities that come with your business. This step takes some more thinking, and you may want to use someone as a sounding board. Again, do not use a friend or a relative who may not be honest with you. No good will come from someone telling you everything is great, that nothing needs to be changed. All businesses have areas where improvements can be made.

Opportunities are created by finding out where your strengths are not being used. How cool is that? These are skills that are already at your disposal, but that are not being utilized. Find out what those opportunities are. Doing so is a simple way to move your company forward.

The Threats

The final S.W.O.T. component is threats. These are things that could hurt your home-based business. Dealing with threats also means looking at things that could become problems. For example, can your ideas, products, or services easily be copied by your competition? Once you are saturating the market with your great marketing strategy, beware of new threats from the competition. As much as you want their clients, they want to keep them even more. By examining threats before they become problems, you will be ahead of the competition already.

Staying in Focus

So how exactly do you keep within the focus of your business? If you position your company as the IT expert in everything, no one will know whether to call if their home computer broke or if their network of 500 computers is down. Define your position in the marketplace and stick to it. Many readers may get wide-eyed when they read this, but turn down jobs that are not in your area of focus. Starting out, people can't believe the suggestion that not all opportunities are good opportunities. When you are approached by a potential client, ask yourself these questions:

"Does this opportunity fit within my scope of work?" It is one thing to stretch yourself out of your comfort zone, it is quite another to take a job that has a steep learning curve and is beyond what you wanted to offer in the first place. For instance, using the IT business example again, if you are positioning yourself as the answer to big business computer problems, taking a job helping Sammy Sanderson fix the home laptop, is not a good use of your time. By the same token, fixing a network of 500 computers may be too big a job for you to handle successfully.

The next questions to ask yourself is, "Will this client need to be walked through the process or are they already market savvy? Will helping them take more time than it is worth?" You need to answer this question to determine how much time you are willing to spend with the client. Your answer will depend on your tolerance and patience to teach potential clients. Spending all your time with one person is not good for you or your business. Client lists are best handled the same as investments: diversify, diversify, diversify.

Lastly, ask yourself, "Does my client baulk at providing a retainer or even discussing costs?" If so, this is a giant red flag. Serious clients will accept the pricing, if you say it confidently and don't start back stepping the moment it comes out of your mouth. People buy products and especially services from people they like as well as trust. Focus your business and build long-term relationships.

Defining Your Goals

Goals should be meaningful, measurable, and specific. Goals give your business something to strive for and achieve. As talked about earlier, you can position your company as being number one, the most respected, or of the highest quality. Now it's time to actually put numbers to paper and write out your marketing goals. While the objective describes what you want your home-based business to be like, setting goals decides what you will reach for through your marketing efforts. The goals of your business can be based on gross revenue, profit, market share, or even the number of clients you serve.

Two Sets of Goals

You should have two sets of goals for your company. Did the word "huh" escape your mouth? Yup, that's right. Two sets of goals. One set that can be reached on a weekly or even daily basis and another set that includes long-term, grabbing for the stars ideas. If you do not learn to stretch yourself and your company by dreaming big, then your company will stay mediocre. If that is where you want to stay, then do not let anyone or anything push you beyond where you are comfortable. But if you want to grow and build your company through your marketing efforts, which is the whole point after all, then stretch for those stars.

Also consider your lifestyle goals as you develop your marketing strategy. If one of the reasons you started your home-based business was to spend more time with your family, use marketing tools and tactics that allow you to attend your child's soccer game. This means, don't schedule a networking event over your priorities.

Make It Meaningful and Personal

What goals are meaningful to you and your business? Personal goals, goals that mean something, sometimes only to you, are the ones that you will most likely achieve. Goals need to include your specific passion. Let's say your goal is to increase your bottom line. That's great, but what makes it personal? Why do you want to increase your bottom line? Is it just to make more money? When the going gets tough, you will need enough reasons not to throw in the towel and give up on your business. What reason are you willing to defend to the death? While the idea of defending something may seem a little extreme, you will need reasons to sustain you through the long haul of building your business. Some personal reasons may include building a business to pass on to your family, having financial freedom, spending more time with your family, buying a house, or buying a new car. Whatever your reasons, make them personal to you. Then pull out that list every time a root canal seems more entertaining than working on your marketing strategy.

Make It Measurable

"Increase the bottom line" is not a measurable goal. However, increasing your revenue by 10 percent and acquiring 15 new accounts per year are great examples of measurable, achievable, goals. Counterpart stretching for the stars goals can be increasing your revenue by 50 percent and gaining 30 new accounts per year. The specific number should matter to you, and it should be a measurable amount. That way you are able to gauge improvement in your home-based business.

There are different types of ways to measure your business's success. You can measure gross revenue, which is the total amount of cash your business takes in during a given time period. If you choose to measure by gross revenue, make sure your number is high enough to cover your operation costs. Another choice is measuring accomplishments by profit, which is the total amount of revenue minus operating costs. Finally, your goals may be measured by your share of the market. However, market share is a little difficult to assess for the home-based business because it might take more research and resources to determine market share than most small home-based businesses have at their disposals. Once you have a way to measure your marketing success and two sets of goals, one that is realistically achievable and one that makes you stretch for the stars, put all your goals on a piece of paper and place it somewhere you can see it every day.

Goals Plus Activity

Besides including your specific passion in your goals, make achieving them a daily process. Achievements are not simply obtained overnight. Steve Jobs of Apple Inc. is credited as stating, "Behind every overnight success is four years of hard work."

Make your stretching for the stars goals specific. Once they are written out, not just thought out, break them down into little tasks you can do on a daily basis. Ask yourself the question, "What am I doing today to achieve my marketing goals?" Even if it is only for 15 minutes a day, do something. Everyone can find 15 minutes a day.

Maybe by playing one less game of Solitaire, surfing one less website, and making one less personal phone call that can wait until nonbusiness hours. The mantra of successful marketing is, say it out loud, "I will market my business on a consistent and persistent basis." Chapter Eight covers setting up your marketing calendar so you can achieve the best results.

Break each goal down. Some goals will take months or even years to accomplish, while others will take less time. Take each goal and determine the time frame in which you want to get it checked off your list. If a particular goal may take years, break it down into meaningful benchmarks so you are encouraged to continue striving to meet the finish line. Determine a reasonable amount of tasks to accomplish each month, each week, and each day to achieve your long-term goals.

Using the example above of increasing your business's revenue by 10 percent and acquiring 15 new clients per year, what must be done to meet those goals? Is it making 20 phone calls a day? Going to a networking event once a week? Is it sending follow-up letters to prospective clients? Could it be finding a graphic designer to develop a direct mailing campaign post card? By being broken down into achievable steps, each goal, whether it is a realistic one or a stretching for the stars one, can be met.

Beware of paralysis when it comes to breaking down your marketing goals. Once your marketing strategy is done, it will become clearer what your goals should be and how you can accomplish them step by step.

Goal Setting Worksheet Example

Definition of Goal	Why do I want to accomplish this goal?	Estimated Completion Date
1. Add five new clients to my business	Increase my income and market share so I can work toward the goal of sending my children to private school	July 31
2. Get 30 people to sign up for my monthly electronic newsletter	Share my knowledge and show potential clients the value of my products or services	August 15
3. Have 20 people attend my seminar presentation	To introduce potential customers to the products or services I offer	September 15
4. Set five one-on-one presentations every week	Meet with potential clients to find out their needs, desires and who they are currently working with and to show them how my business is the answer to their needs, desires, and problems	Every Friday
5. Schedule one training seminar a month	To train customers on the best uses of my products or services	End of every month

Reward Yourself

While working your marketing strategy to reach your ultimate goals, give yourself some rewards along the way. When starting out, you may be using all the marketing tools and tactics that your market research has indicated will appeal to your ideal client, but you might not be getting the results you anticipated. Use this information to change your marketing strategy in the future, but make sure to give yourself some gifts for the work completed to date. Otherwise you will begin feeling like your hard work is not paying off and start spending less and less time on achieving your ultimate goals for your home-based business.

Once you have made your 20 phone calls for the day, finished an article, or done some market research, give yourself a break, and call a friend, read the latest celebrity gossip on the Internet, read the next chapter in a great book, or play your favorite video game. Make your reward something that you believe is worth waiting for, and only give it to yourself after you have finished your marketing tasks for the day. This may sound like the gold star program used in most kindergarten classrooms, but rewarding yourself will keep you going when you don't want to do what needs to be done.

Be Excited

Being a laser beam and knowing your products or services like the back of your hand is essential for establishing your goals and objectives, but even more important is being excited about your business as well as your prospects. You should be excited to share the ideas your business represents because excitement is contagious. Remember the last person who told you about a fabulous restaurant? Based on their excitement you had a greater desire to visit the place.

Marketing your wares will be difficult some days, and if you are not excited about your business, no one else will be either. It is sometimes a lonely road and it may become difficult to continue your pursuit to the one "yes, please" among all the "no, thanks." On those days when you are having a tough time, find a motivator around you that can bolster you and get you back on track to meeting your business goals and objectives. Your passion for your products or services will translate into enthusiastic marketing.

The Fear Factor

The thought of defining your objectives, setting your goals, or even starting your daily tasks may leave some of you with sweaty palms, shaky knees, and the feeling of having cotton balls in your mouth. While these are classic examples of being nervous, genuine fear could keep you from working on your marketing strategy. This could be a fear of failure, disappointment, or even success.

Overcoming Fear

When writing out your goals and your reasons for wanting your home-based business to succeed, think about the cost of failure. Many people want to push this idea aside and not even give failure a foothold in their minds, but determining the cost of failure may push you to work even harder and set your goals higher. If you fail at this home-based business, what are the consequences? Will you not be able to pay for a place to live? Will you still be able to put food on your table? Have you mortgaged your house to the limit for this business and if it fails you will lose your home? Would you lose the respect of your family, friends, or former coworkers? When you want to file paperwork, do laundry, or catch the latest television show instead of working on your marketing strategy, think about what failure could cost you and remember the two sets of goals you have created for your home-based business.

The first step to overcoming your fear is to imagine yourself reaching your goals and to imagine yourself not reaching your goals. Which is a scarier scenario? If reaching your goals creates more fear than not reaching your goals, every day, before you start using your marketing tools, create an image of success in your mind. Imagine yourself reaching all your goals and enjoying the better life you have created by doing so. If you want to redecorate your home office once you attain one of your marketing goals, motivate yourself by putting up pictures of beautiful home offices that you would like to emulate. If your reward will be to buy a new car, post a picture of the car you want where you can see it every day. If your goal is to make a $50,000 sale, make a check out to yourself in the amount of $50,000 and, once again, place it where you can see it all the time. Whenever you feel like skipping out on your marketing strategy, use these objects as motivators to make the next call, write the next sales letter, or create the next presentation.

The second step is to listen to the negative comments people are aiming at you or your home-based business.

While you are often told to just ignore negative comments, they can help you improve and grow your business, so examine each one. Does the comment have any validity? Where is the person's motive for the comment coming from? Are they a true friend who is watching your back or are they jealous that you are on the road to success? What if the negative comment is coming from you?

The third step to overcoming your fear is to keep the positive voice inside you at the loudest level so it tunes out any negative messages you may be sending yourself. How do you do that? By using positive self-talk. Create a list of statements in the present tense that will help you accomplish your marketing goals. Then use them on a daily basis, saying them out loud and, if possible, in front of a mirror. Your statements could be simple, such as:

- People are attracted to my business.
- Clients seek out my advice and pay me well for it.
- I have a monthly advice column that helps people as well as showcases my talents and abilities.
- I earn over $100,000 a year.
- I am an entertaining and funny public speaker.

Once again, make these statements meaningful and personal to you. Remember, you will go where you think you will go. Make your thoughts positive and watch your marketing tools achieve extraordinary results.

The fourth step is to find friends, business partners, or coaches to help you maintain your progress. Surrounding yourself with people who want to see you succeed will be your greatest asset in the goal setting process. Find people who want to help you, but will also be honest with you about your progress and the practicality of your tasks. It is also fantastic to have someone celebrate your accomplishments with you.

Be Committed

Creating a marketing strategy with specific, measurable goals is the right start for your business. If need be, determine which goals are most important for your home-based business at this exact time to avoid feeling overwhelmed. Regardless, you must be dedicated to achieving the objectives and goals you have put in place. It is a disservice to your business and your clients if you are not 100 percent committed. Vince Lombardi, the great coach of the Green Bay Packers, said, "Winning isn't everything – it's the only thing." How bad do you want to reach your version of success? Use your list of objectives and goals as a road map to help you reach business success, whatever your definition of it is.

Final Thoughts

By doing a little bit of work on your marketing strategy each day, you will be living the mantra of being consistent and persistent. In the long run, the result will be a thriving business that will meet or even exceed all your objectives and goals.

3 DESCRIBING YOUR PRODUCTS
OR SERVICES

Remember as a kid when people would ask, "What do you want to be when you grow up?" More than likely you had an enthusiastic answer ready to be shouted at anyone who would listen. Think of describing your products or services in the same way. When anyone asks about your business, have an enthusiastic response ready. Your initial excitement about your products or services along with a cohesive description may mean the difference between a sale and people walking away empty-handed.

The last thing any home-based business owner wants is to lose out on a potential sale or a long-term client because they were not prepared to answer the question, "So what do you do?" Your business is more than your 10-second introduction, which is covered later in this chapter, and it is more than your tagline or slogan, but you need to create a succinct message that lets your potential customers know what you can do to help them.

Developing your USP or your Unique Selling Position will make it clear not only in your mind, but in the minds of your potential customers why they should buy from you rather than from your competition. Before you begin marketing, or revamping your marketing, have your customer in mind.

Having an understanding of your USP will make your life easier when people start questioning you about your products or services. Since you will have already done your homework, you will be able to answer all their objections before they can even think of them.

The USP is the core of your marketing message. Every marketing tool you use should encapsulate your USP. If you don't have a common message and theme throughout your marketing materials, your efforts as well as your results will be haphazard. So how do you develop a USP?

<u>Defining the Products or Services</u>

Once again, you must ask yourself questions about your products or services. These are questions that you can answer by yourself or with a team. However, it is ultimately your business, and the final answers to these questions should come from you. While answering these, keep in mind that a USP is not about what you want or think is great about your products or services; it's about what your target market wants from your products or services.

What need are your products or services meeting in the marketplace?

What do your products or services mean to you?

Why are you offering your products or services?

How do they help your target market?

What are the features of your products or services?

Will they make your target market richer, prettier, safer, or healthier?

Will they save your target market time or money?

Do they make their lives easier or bring them more pleasure? How?

How or when should your products or services be used?

Are they renewable? That is, do clients need to use them again and again? If not, how can you make them that way? Or what do your products or services offer that keep your clients coming back for more?

Why should people buy from you and not from your competition?

How does your USP motivate customers to act now? Is it price? A limited time offer? Is it a free gift with purchase?

If it is difficult for a potential client to figure out what you do, they will not take the time to figure it out. Time is a precious commodity and your potential customers need to see the benefits of your products or services immediately before they will use their time to investigate further.

What many business owners get wrong in their marketing is thinking they know what people need from their products or services. A customer's reality is based on their perception, not necessarily on what really happens. This means what a person needs is an answer to what they perceive as a problem. Pin point how your products or services alleviate their problems or save them time and money. If you cannot figure out why people need your products or services, then they'll be dead in the water before you spend your first marketing dollar.

The description of the products or services your home-based business offers must be precise and concise. People have a limited attention span for marketing messages. Think of your customers as three-year-olds who ate about 10 Pixy Stixs each. Because your potential customers are inundated with marketing messages every second of every day, the description of your products or services needs to convey how it will help them, immediately and concisely.

Describe your products or services by their features. When the uniqueness of your business combines with your business's ability to satisfy the needs of your customer, your products or services become a benefit that the customer can't get anywhere else, setting you apart from your competition.

<u>Price</u>

Knowing how you are different from your competition helps you determine your price. Once your products or services are unique, you can take the first step in your pricing: setting your price on perceived value rather than on actual cost.

To do this, consider how much it will cost you to produce and bring your products or services to market. If you price yourself too low, you won't be able to cover your costs, but if you price yourself too high, you won't be able to get clients. If you can offer something that no one else can, then you can charge whatever you want.

Finding out how much people are willing to pay for your products or services can be tricky because potential clients normally say they will only pay the lowest amount. If you work with your local Small Business Administration office or Small Business Development Center, they may help you put together a focus group, which will cost less than hiring a marketing consultant firm. You can also conduct your own research by using the Internet, the phone, or mail. Specific research methods are covered in Chapter Four. When working with a research group, don't ask them what they would be willing to pay for your products or services, ask them what they would pay for your products or services in a store if they needed them.

<u>Reasons for Buying</u>

There are a few basic reasons people will buy your products or services. The first is pleasure. They will buy your products or services if they can enjoy them. They will buy if the products or services you offer make their lives easier by saving them time, reducing their stress, or making them feel better. Tap into how what you are offering grants your potential clients a pleasurable experience.

The second reason people will buy is for profit. They will buy if doing so will increase their rate of success or the possibility of their being successful. Also, because the cost of living is increasing at a sometimes dramatic rate, most people, unless they have more money than they know what to do with, want to save money. If buying from you will save people money, then use your USP to drive home that aspect. If your target market does include people who have more money than they know what to do with, though, do not try to sell them on price. They want to be sold on service, opportunity, and exclusivity.

Pride is the third factor that motivates people to buy. Otherwise known as keeping up with the Joneses, pride is more of a selling point for those who have discretionary incomes. When Fred down the street has the newest gadget, then, by golly, his neighbor should have one too. Use your USP to create urgency in having the newest, greatest thing to hit the marketplace if you want to sell people on pride.

Pain is the fourth factor that creates sales. If your products or services can reduce potential customers' pain or if your products or services can cause pain, people will buy them. Meaning, if it will cause your potential clients more pain not to have your products or not to use your services than it will to buy them, people will want them. Make your potential customers realize the cost of not doing business with you and that by not acting immediately they will be bringing more pain into their lives.

Help your target market see better benefits with you than with your competition. Use all the marketing tools in your marketing strategy to bring potential clients to say "Yes." This means, at each point of contact, reiterate how your products or services will benefit them. Show them purchasing from you is an investment in a better life.

If you are thinking to yourself, "Geez, I am only selling a widget. Does it really matter if it will change someone's life?" The answer is an overwhelming, "Yes!" People only buy products or services if they will benefit their lives in some way. Touch on that point within your target market, and sales will follow.

Placement

The placement of your products or services is critical when describing them. The whole point of marketing is getting your products into the hands of your target market, and thinking about placement is important in doing so. Will you be offering your products through retail, mail order, a distributor, personal selling, direct response, or the Internet? Which of these, or which combination of these distribution channels will be the easiest way to deliver your products? Are you going to need storage for them?

Though services are placed differently, the concept is the same. When you operate a service business, you may not need to get your products into storefronts, but you need to get your foot in the door with your target market by placing yourself where your target market is likely to be. For example, if you are a wedding planner, a great place to put your business cards or to offer a wedding planning prep class is at a local jewelry store.

Find a place where your products or services will stand out from the crowd. For example, take a beef jerky sales booth. The first time, its owner opened it in a trade show emphasizing specialty foods. It turned out to be one of ten other beef jerky booths at the trade show. The next trade shows its owner attended was an outdoor sports show. This time, the booth was the only beef jerky booth in the entire place. There were three lines three to four people deep at any given time of the day. Have a unique offering while meeting your target market where they are and placement will become another benefit for your customers.

Get Them Hooked

A hook is a statement or message that immediately grabs people's attentions. Keep your prospects' attentions by developing a hook. Think about those late night infomercials. They immediately get you interested by showing the body you have always dreamed of, and then the announcer says, "Do you want rock-hard abs in less than eight minutes a day?" Of course you do, but you think, "Could it really only take eight minutes a day?" Your curiosity gets the best of you so you keep watching. Then you're hooked.

Creating a hook is as simple as asking a "Yes" question or making a statement that your target market can identify with. The hook of your products or services should come from your core marketing message. Because it is difficult to convince your target market they need something when they do not know they need it, the hook should immediately state how your home-based business fulfills a perceived need or solves a problem. Your hook must also bypass the hesitation factor people have when they consider purchasing things.

Personalize It

You can have more than one target market, but make sure to develop each thoroughly. If you are aiming for more than one target market, customize your marketing message to achieve the best results in each category. For example, let's say your home-based business helps people get organized. Your target markets are busy professionals who cannot keep their homes or offices organized, and homeowners who just want to keep their homes organized. One of the marketing tools in your strategy could be writing articles to drive prospects to your website where they can sign up for your newsletter or get free quotes on your organizational services. So when you write an article, you can submit it to online article banks under two different headings. First, hook the professional business crowd with the question, "Are you losing sales because you keep losing phone numbers, contracts, or files?" Then proceed to offer tips on keeping the office organized. Then, submit the article again, this time with the question, "When was the last time you actually ate at your kitchen table rather than used it as a horizontal filing cabinet?" Proceed to offer the same, slightly modified, organizational tips as in the previous article. This way, you get articles that fit both your target markets without twice the work or the expense.

Creating Your Tagline or Slogan

Working through some of your potential clients' hesitations can be done before you even meet them. While some of this is accomplished through image and design, which is covered in Chapter Six, you can also help close the sale through your tagline or slogan. Your tagline or slogan should come from your core marketing message.

Before you can create a tagline or a slogan, you will need to work through the questions in the beginning of the chapter. Answer these questions for your customers or your competitor will. Being bombarded with marketing messages from huge corporations on a daily basis makes it difficult for people to notice home-based businesses. Make it easy for your potential client to close the sale by clearly conveying the benefits your products or services will provide them.

Once again, it's not about how you think your products or services will satisfy their needs, it's about how your target market thinks they will. For most people, their reality is based on their perception, not necessarily on what is really there. Look at the reality of your target market and aim your marketing message to address their needs based on that reality.

<u>Introducing Your Products or Services</u>

In a matter of seconds, you should be able to explain what you do and how it benefits people, while including the name of your company. Developing a 10-second introduction, and rehearsing it so it flows naturally, is another key to building your business because, once again, in an over marketed world, people have shoddy attention spans. (Remember the three-year-old who ate too many Pixy Stixs?) Be short and to the point and covey your benefits in seconds and people will want to know more. If someone doesn't want to know more, then they are not your ideal client anyway, and you should tactfully move on to the next person. So what does a 10-second introduction that encompasses all these traits look like? Glad you asked.

Here are a few examples:

"My name is Sally Wilson. I crush people's fears. I am a phobia psychologist and my company is Rout Your Fear."

"My name is Bill Kay. I create green ideas for purple thumbs. I am a landscape architect and my company is All About Land."

These companies are fictitious, but you get the idea: provide your name, express a benefit, give your title, and state your company name in under 10 seconds, and if you can, in under five.

Now Time For a Commercial Break

Your 10-second introduction should pique the interest of your audience. If it works and they want to know more about your products or services, pull out your 30-second commercial, otherwise known as an elevator speech.

Use these 30 seconds wisely because what you say about your products or services when you first meet someone in your target market could make or break the sale. Do not leave it up to chance. Have something prepared and rehearse it out loud, preferably in front of a mirror.

Think about those 30-second commercials that run every year during the Super Bowl. At millions of dollars for a single advertising spot and with the whole world watching, companies develop creative ways to talk about the products or services they have to offer. While as a home-based business owner, you probably don't have the advertising budget of a corporation, it doesn't mean you can't emulate them when talking about your contributions to the business world.

The 30 seconds you have with a potential client need to succinctly cover what your home-based business does, and hopefully with a memorable story attached to it. Most people remember and relate to stories better than they do to tutorials and anything of the like. In your 30-second spot, include some of the benefits associated with your products or services and how those benefits could help the person you are speaking with. While you might not have enough specific information on the person you are talking to, as discussed earlier in the chapter, there are universal benefits that apply to many, so include points that touch on pleasure, profit, pride, and pain in your 30 seconds.

The final step in your 30-second blurb is to ask for a follow-up meeting if the person wants more information. Many home-based business owners avoid this because they are scared of rejection. But by letting you get past your 10-second introduction, the person has shown an interest in you as well as in your business. Think about the absolute worst thing that can happen if they say no to any more information. It probably won't be as bad as you think it will. Think about the best case scenario if they say yes, and focus on that outcome rather than on the possibility of hearing the word "no."

You may deviate from your practiced script based on the

needs of the person you are talking to; just make sure you have something memorable to say when people want more information. Leaving people with a favorable impression, not only of you, but of your products or services can mean the difference between people taking your call in the future or letting it repeatedly go to voicemail after checking the caller ID.

Overcoming Objections

Make it so simple for your target market to say yes that they have a hard time saying no. Doing this means answering their objections before they can even think of them. Think about every possible objection and have a counter to it before your ideal client can even mention it. Then address the objections in your marketing collateral. Whether it is on your website, in your printed marketing collateral, or in your presentation, address objections your target market has against your business.

As an example, let's say you own a home-based cleaning business. While people may know the benefits of having someone else clean their homes, such as having more time with family, reduced stress, and a cleaner home environment, many do not hire a cleaning service because of the objections they have, such as feeling the need to clean their houses before the cleaning crew arrives so they aren't judged on just how messy they are, having safety concerns about someone being in their houses while they are not there, and wondering what they should do if they believe the cleaning crew broke something or ruined a piece of furniture because of their cleaning methods. These are just a few objections that come to people's minds when they are thinking about hiring someone to clean their homes. How could a cleaning business overcome these objections?

Take the concern of feeling the need to clean before the cleaning crew arrives. In your marketing materials, let people know that no matter the state of their houses, your company is there to help. You may even make it funny by doing a before and after picture in your literature that shows a garbage dump as the before image and a sparkling clean house as the after, with the tagline, "If you think your place is bad, you should see some of our previous clients'. We offer no judgment cleaning services."

To address the concern of broken or stolen things, you could notify potential customers that you are bonded and insured, and provide them with the names of your satisfied clients, whom they can call to inquire about your service practices. If you aren't speaking to potential clients directly and it is your collateral doing the talking, include testimonial statements and an offer to provide more if necessary. Just knowing you are willing to share names makes people feel at ease.

If your potential client brings up an objection that hasn't been addressed in your marketing collateral, listen to every word of their objection without interrupting. Once they are finished speaking, rephrase the concern and repeat it to them so they know you heard and understood their problem. If you need more clarification about their concern, this is the time to ask questions to find out what it will take to allay their fear. Once you know, link the benefits of your products or services to their concerns.

Finally, get confirmation that their objection has been addressed. If there is another concern, go through the process again.

If all their objections have been addressed, ask whether there is any other reason that would prevent them from buying from you. This may feel like a used car salesman line, but the biggest mistake most people make is not going for the sale at the closing of answering all the objections. By asking if they have any more concerns they will realize they don't, and consider making the purchase.

Do not send mixed messages about who you are or what your stand for. Not only do you need to be consistent and persistent in your marketing efforts, but you need to be consistent and persistent with your marketing message, especially when addressing objections.

Getting Customers to Act

One of the travesties of marketing is that some people think the main purpose of developing a USP is creating product awareness. But product awareness doesn't put money in the bank or offer any return on your marketing investment. Getting customers to buy your products or services is the biggest indicator the USP and marketing tools are working. How do you get potential clients to become right-now clients? By offering them something they can't refuse.

What is the one thing about your products or services people cannot live without? Why is it that? Now, make your potential customers act by creating an irresistible offer. This could be a discount for all new clients, a free gift with purchase, or even a free consultation.

Your offer can be whatever you want it to be. Once you've created it, you can place it on the back of your business card so when people meet you for the first time they are aware of the offer. You can also place it on the front page of your website, or the two could work together. For example, let's say you meet a potential client at a networking event and they are very interested in your products or services. On the back of your business card, you have the offer of a free newsletter on organization tips for homes and offices for those who visit your website. In that newsletter make special offers on a monthly basis to entice potential clients to work with you. By doing these things, you will continually be making a connection with the potential buyer, and they will know where to turn in their time of need.

<u>Final Thoughts</u>

When developing the USP, tagline, slogan, or any marketing message for your home-based business, remember two things: The first is that you are offering something better than your competition, so make it show. Determining what sets you apart and how you can make that apparent through marketing messages in every marketing tool you incorporate will place you light-years ahead of others.

The second is to treat your potential clients or customers with respect when presenting your marketing messages. Think of them as if they are your mother, father, brother, sister, best friend, or significant other. Keep in mind how you would want that special person treated by others when developing your marketing message. How would you want a company to approach them? Probably with as much respect for their time, intelligence, and needs as you would want to be treated with.

As a home-based business owner the buck should stop with you. Determine what marketing message you can stand behind. Are you willing to put your reputation on the line for your USP, tagline, slogan, and special offers? Since you are your home-based business, final buying decisions are based on you and the relationship you build with your potential clients.

4 DEFINING YOUR TARGET MARKET AND DEVELOPING YOUR IDEAL CUSTOMER PROFILE

Finding a target market, otherwise known as your niche, is the best way for a home-based business to effectively utilize its marketing dollars. When businesses take the spaghetti approach to marketing--throwing noodles on the wall and seeing what sticks--they might as well start burning the dollars in their marketing budgets. Become a lean, mean marketing machine by doing some homework before you spend $600 on an advertisement in a magazine that no one in your target market will read or $400 on a set of post cards that will sit in a closet because you have no idea where to send them.

Hitting the Bulls'-Eye

Developing a target market means making the bull's-eye bigger by narrowing down each category. When you hit the sweet spot over and over again, that is when the sales will start rolling. While market research is not the most entertaining part of developing a marketing plan, it is essential.

For example, a technology company wanted to ramp up their marketing, so they considered hiring a great marketing person who specialized in graphic design and in compiling statistical data from geographical information systems. The marketing consultant could then give the technology company a database to send the beautifully created graphic materials to. This sounded like a good plan to the technology company until they realized that they had no idea where or who to send their marketing collateral to because they didn't know if their ideal target market would be based on a geographical area, financial status, age, or gender. It was a classic case of the spaghetti approach.

Before they hired someone to create beautiful marketing collateral or even to generate a database, they researched their ideal target market by using the methods described in this chapter. By doing that, they didn't have a set of marketing brochures collecting dust in their office because they didn't appeal to their potential clients. They focused their marketing efforts and targeted other businesses that could use their services.

By defining how and who you are helping, you can narrow down your possible target market. If you are struggling with this, go back and reread Chapter Three, which discusses describing your products or services.

Questions

Since most home-based businesses have limited marketing budgets, it is essential to ask yourself questions about how and who your products or services will benefit. Your target demographic is the people who are profiled as needing your products or services the most. The more information you have on them, the better your decisions will be which means a thicker, blacker bottom line. What does your ideal client look like? Start by asking yourself the following questions:

Demographics:

Are they male or female?

What is their age?

Where do they live?

What do they live in? Is it a single family residence, a townhouse, an apartment, etc.?

Do they live alone, do they live with family, or do they have a roommate?

Where do they work? How far is their commute?

What is their household income?

Psychographics:

Imagine what your ideal client likes to do in their spare time.

How do they spend their time?

Is it watching or playing sports?

Seeing a movie in their home theater or at the theater?

Reading by going to the library or the book store or by downloading?

Think about what they like to eat and drink.

Do they eat at fast-food places, at home, or at sit-down restaurants?

What do they drink?

Are they addicted to Starbucks, Coke, Pepsi, Red Bull, or Gatorade?

Think about where they shop.

Is a low price important to them, so they shop at Wal-Mart?

Are they hip and shop at Target?

Are they all about excellent service and shop at Nordstrom?

What are their families like?

Are they parents?

What age are their children?

Do they work outside the home?

Do they really want to stay at home with the kids?

Do they really want to get out of the house and away from the kids?

It is the age of the child that matters most when relating to customers with children. Parents of all ages with small children are dealing with sleep deprivation, teething, and potty training while parents of teenagers are thinking about peer pressure and keeping kids away from drugs and alcohol, as well as preparing them for college, trade school, or a job.

Breaking down the general population into your target markets works like this: Let's say you have a beauty product that reverses the signs of aging. This product is ideal for men or women, but women are more likely to use the product. The women who normally want to use anti-aging products are over the age of 30, and more likely between the ages of 40 and 70. They have disposable incomes that can be spent on beauty products, are concerned about their appearance, and have the time to devote to using the products consistently.

Free or Low-Cost Market Research

Once you have a general idea of what kind of potential customers will benefit the most from your business offerings and how, it is time to do some research. Get as much information as possible about the demographic you are targeting. There is a wealth of information available for free or for a small fee, so there is no excuse not to research your target market. The rest of this chapter covers ways a home-based business owner can research their ideal client for free or for a low cost.

The Library

Before you start surfing the Internet, only to get sidetracked by the latest sports scores or celebrity gossip, start researching at your local library. There are these great people there whose job it is to help you find stuff. Really! If your vision of a librarian includes an old woman telling you to be quiet and to stop turning the pages so loudly, envision the new library system. Most libraries, even in small towns, have librarians who are dedicated to researching and finding information that you need, for free. Well, it's not totally free; your tax dollars are at work, so make them work for you.

Tell the librarian, nicely, what you are looking for and watch them go to work with you. This does not mean they will do all the work while you sit in the corner with an illegal food and drink, but they can point you in the right direction, to reference books, statistical data, and periodicals. Look through the materials and find trends in society. Some developments in recent years are the aging of the baby boomers, the continued rise of home-based businesses, and the movement of members in society. These are not the only trends in society, so find out what is going on and decide how your products or services fit into these developments.

Once you find resources from working with a librarian, use one of the free information databases most libraries have on their websites. Normally, you just need a valid library card to access the databases.

The Internet

Now you can start surfing the Internet in search of more information about your target market. Different top pages pop up on most search engines so it pays to conduct multiple searches, but stick with the big search engines (Google, Bing, Yahoo, Lycos) because the smaller ones repeat the data of the larger ones.

Government Resources

You can also use the Internet for free information from your local, regional, or national government agencies. Once again, your hard-earned tax dollars are already paying for free information from the government. Organizations such as the Census Bureau, the Bureau of Labor and Statistics, The White House, and the Department of Commerce all have a wealth of information on the Internet that is not only free, but that is not copyrighted, so you can plunder away at your heart's content.

The following websites are great places to obtain current statistics:

- U.S. Census Bureau - www.census.gov
- Bureau of Labor and Statistics - stats.bls.gov
- Federal Government Statistics - http://www.whitehouse.gov/briefing-room

Trade and Professional Associations

When you are researching business to business marketing and you need information on a certain industry, look for trade or professional associations. There is an association for just about every industry in existence, so use the search engines mentioned above to look for any association involved, even peripherally, in your target industry market.

Using the Phone

Another way to obtain information is through the telephone. Use an Internet directory, some are Dexonline.com or Yellowbook.com, to create a wordplay on a popular slogan--let your fingers do the dialing. Find businesses or individuals who are part of your target market and give them a call. Remember, you are not trying to sell them anything because if you are, you may be betraying the regulations of the "no call" list. But, if you are calling to do research, the "no call" list regulations do not apply. A sample questionnaire can be found in the Appendix. Using the phone is a great source for information because it allows you to mine data from your potential target market.

Snail Mail

If you want more original research, you can create a mail survey for your potential market. While the return rate of a mail survey is relatively low, you can increase your chances of a return by making the survey on a preaddressed, postage paid post card and offering a small prize for the return of the mail survey. Not only will a post card save you money on postage, but it has a higher rate of return than standard letter format. While e-mail is a free option for doing a survey, e-mails are easy to delete, and you may be blacklisted as a spammer, so be careful before going this route.

Interviews

A great way of obtaining first-hand information is through the interview process. This means contacting people in your target market and asking them out for coffee or lunch and picking their brain about what they need in products or services similar to yours. Even though people are busy, most are willing to get a free coffee or meal and talk about themselves for a little while. You never know, during the information gathering process, they may become your first client.

Chamber of Commerce

Use your local chamber of commerce to get information on your target market. Most chambers have websites from which you can get information, such as business listings for their members, for free. Give them a call and find out what resources are available to nonmembers and what services they offer for free or for a low cost. You might have to sit through a sales pitch, but the information could help you further narrow your target market, and that will save you money in the long run.

Focus Groups

Using a focus group is an excellent way to test your products or services before taking them to market. A focus group is a set of hopefully unbiased individuals who are part of your target market. Even home-based business owners have access to focus groups without parting with their limited marketing dollars. Contact a Small Business Development Center, Small Business Administration, or even your local chamber of commerce to see if they conduct focus groups. Some organizations will run them for free, while others have a minimum charge associated with the service. This is also great for testing possible offers as well as design ideas.

<u>Testing, Testing, 1, 2, 3, Testing</u>

A word of caution, even products or services with the most research behind them, should be given small test runs before being launched in full-blown marketing campaigns. An example of why comes from the U.S.A. Olympic Track and Field Team. When one-hundredth of a second means going home with the gold metal or going home empty-handed, the competition to find the best gear is vital. Scientists developed a new running outfit with a hood that reduced wind resistance. The lab results and the outdoor field results were great, so it was adopted as part of the uniform for the track squad. Unfortunately, there was one complication: during the relay race, when the hoods were up, runners receiving the batons couldn't hear the other runners from behind so they started late and dropped the batons. Even though the research and testing showed great potential, the practical application was a failure. Make sure what you are offering will work in the real world.

Now that you have assembled all this great information, how do you use it? The answer: to build the perfect customer profile. The typical ideal client is broken down by age, gender, and location.

Having a vision of your ideal client will enable you to work with people who are in your ideal market. This will make closing the sale easier because, as you learned from your research and test marketing, these people want and need your products or services.

Potential Clients

The vision of the ideal client makes it easier to qualify a potential customer. When starting out in a home-based business, it is easy to get lost chasing after false leads or holding one lead out as the home run. While the home run may materialize, it is important to keep filling the pipeline with qualified leads that could be base hits which tide your business over until the home run comes to fruition. However, it is a waste of your time to work a purchased phone list or a mailing list without first qualifying the prospects. Do the people or businesses on the list meet the criteria for your ideal client? If they do, then you need to ask them some qualifying questions to see how serious they are about the products or services you offer. Some examples include:

How soon do you need the products or services?

What are your other options?

Are you talking to anyone else?

If I answer your objections today, are you willing to buy from me?

Listen, Listen, Listen

Listen to the answers your potential client gives. Similar to real estate where everything is about location, location, location, when meeting with someone, whether they are going to buy from you or not, listen, listen, listen. Even if they don't become one of your customers, they can talk to their friends, family, and business associates about the great meeting they had with you.

When you are speaking with your ideal client, do not think about what your next move is or about the next question on the form. Really listen. There is a reason you were given two ears and one mouth. Listening is rare these days. At a time when people are checking their cell phones, Blackberries, or iPhones every two minutes for a message, it makes a difference when you make eye contact and respond to what a person is saying or doing.

Be an Effective Listener

Now that you're listening, do so as best as you can. It cannot be stressed enough how important it is to listen to potential customers, and existing customers for that matter. Beyond being able to answer objections and respond to their needs, you will be able to establish a connection with them, which could lead to long-term relationships with you and your business. People who listen to others are extremely effective in their businesses because their interest in what potential customers have to say is evident.

Make Eye Contact

To be an effective listener, and in turn a better marketer, there are a few actions you can do, such as making eye contact. When you are listening to someone, unless you are writing something down, look them in the eye. It makes the person feel heard, and they will respond more positively to your overall message.

Mirror, Mirror, on the Wall

Another way to make a person feel heard is by mirroring–that is, by imitating their movements. This isn't like what you did to annoy your siblings growing up. You are following potential customers' movements enough to make them feel at ease, but not enough to make them feel like your brother or sister when you teased them.

Rephrase

Rephrasing what the person said to you is also a mark of a successful listener. Don't parrot the person, but when they are explaining a problem they have with your products or services, after they are finished talking start with, "So what I hear you saying is…" and then restate the objection or comment along with your answer. This may feel weird at first, but you will learn to listen better and in turn develop deeper relationships.

Take Notes

Listening effectively is not just about making eye contact, mirroring the other person, and rephrasing their concerns or comments, it also involves visual cues. To listen effectively, be ready to take notes in your meeting. Taking notes is a visual cue that you are ready to listen.

When talking to potential clients, listen to your gut, intuition, or whatever your reality check is. People give off nonverbal signals. If you can tell they are really not interested, do not waste your time or theirs by dragging out a meeting or phone call in hopes of convincing them to purchase your products or services. Chalk it up to a lesson learned, and move on to a better qualified client. Your marketing time is precious; do not waste it on an unqualified customer.

Presenting to Your Ideal Client

Now that you have a vision of your ideal client it is time to think about how to make the best presentation possible to reach your ultimate goal--to close the deal. One of the biggest mistakes business owners can make is assuming that since they know their products or services so well, they can just wing their presentations. Nothing could be further from the truth. While you have a general outline of your ideal client, you are presenting to an individual person with different needs, desires, and hot-button issues than the next person. Before making your sales presentation to someone in your target market, think about what will appeal most to that person.

It's Environmental

What kind of environment are you meeting in? Is it casual or professional? As the saying goes, you only have one chance to make a first impression. Let your first impression be a positive one by planning to put your prospect at ease. Mimic how your contact is dressed. If you are overdressed for the occasion, your prospect may feel uncomfortable. If you are underdressed, however, your prospect may think you are not professional enough for the job. When the place you are meeting at gives you no clues on the attire your prospect may be wearing, dress more professionally rather than casually.

Be Genuine

Approach your contact with a smile and a firm handshake. Above all focus on the needs of your prospect and be genuine. People can sense if you're a phony as soon as you enter the room. Break the ice by asking questions that have nothing to do with the business at hand. Along with trying to make the sale, you are trying to build a relationship. Be sincere when you are interacting with a potential client; otherwise, you will be doing more harm than good for your business.

Keep the Goal in Mind

When discussing your products or services, keep in mind that your goal is getting the prospect to sign on the dotted line. This means using small yes questions to get to the final "yes." Using yes questions means listing the benefits of your products or services and asking if your prospect needs or could use the benefit. The scary part is your prospect could say "no." If they do, it is up to you to decide whether this is a client to whom you want to present other benefits or whether you should cut your losses, thank your prospect for their time, and move on to the next person.

Be Prepared

The more preparation you put in your presentation, the more confident you will be in what your home-based business has to offer. Know what objections your ideal client may have before you even meet with them and have answers prepared for those objections. As stated earlier, enthusiasm is contagious, but confidence is just as important, and being confident in your products or services leads your ideal client to be confident in you.

Come Out, Come Out Wherever You Are

You have researched your target market, described what your ideal client looks like, and prepared a knockout presentation--now where do you find the clients? Normally, customers don't beat down your doorstep when you open your home-based business. Therefore, it is imperative to go where your potential market is, where you can build relationships with different people.

Family and Friends

A great place to start finding clients is within your family and friends. Some of you may be saying, my family and friends don't need my graphic design services or my writing services or the business copier I am selling. While that may be the case, the companies they work for just might need all those things. The point is to let them know what you do. Most family and friends want to see you succeed and are more than willing to help you out. If this is not the case, find a new set of friends immediately. Contact them and give them your 30-second elevator speech; ask them if they or anyone else they know might be in need of your products or services. If you are scared of presenting to a complete stranger at a networking event, presenting to those you know is a great place to start building up your confidence.

Make It Personal

If you take classes for fun or for personal development,

whether it is at a local college, at an art center, or at your local gym, you have a place where you could meet ideal clients. Sharing common interests with people is a great way to begin a relationship and share what you do for a living.

The Kids

For home-based business owners with kids, there is a whole other market for reaching potential clients. This doesn't mean you should give your children marketing literature and have them hand it out on your behalf. However, having kids normally means you meet other parents through play dates, organizations for parents and kids, and school events, as well as through extracurricular activities. Involving kids in soccer, piano, voice lessons, dance classes, and art classes every week has become standard practice these days. While you may be putting hundreds of miles on your car shuttling your children to these different appointments, each class has a new set of parents for you to meet and build relationships with. You never know who needs what in this world, so don't be afraid to tell people what you do.

Neighbors

If your neighbors aren't part of your friend network, but you are friendly with them, they are still a great place to tap into your target market. As a home-based business owner, you are now in the neighborhood, generally, most of the day. On snowy or rainy days, your car may not move from its appointed location and your neighbors will begin to notice, unless you live in a place where public transportation is the norm. Your neighbors may begin to wonder what you are doing home all day. Let them know about your home-based business and give them your 10-second introduction or even your 30-second commercial.

Religious Organizations

Now, don't go and join a church just to meet potential customers, but if you attend a church, a synagogue, or another religious establishment regularly, you may be able to find clients through the network of people that you meet. If you are in the services industry, you may be able to share your expertise with your religious organization, not only as a way of helping others but as a way of establishing yourself as an expert in your industry within your community.

Former Coworkers

Unless you are starting your home-based business at a young age, you probably had a previous job or career before starting your business. Now, if you left your previous job by packing up your stuff and telling your boss to take his job and shove it while being escorted to the exit by a security guard, you probably won't have any potential clients there. However, if you are welcome and are still in the same field, this is a great market to tap into. You could approach your former company about being a consultant, or if your home-based business focuses on product sales to individuals, you could approach your former coworkers about your new home-based business.

Chamber of Commerce

Not only will your local chamber of commerce help you

with gathering information on your ideal client, chambers of commerce also exist to help businesses and people find other businesses and people who need what they are offering. You pay a fee, normally based on the size of your business, to attend networking events, luncheons, breakfasts, and lead groups with the intent of meeting people to do business with. Make sure to check out a chamber before joining. Find out if there are extra fees to attend their events, what events they offer on a regular basis, if they offer the use of conference rooms for home-based businesses, and what their member demographic is. Most chambers have a free online list of members, so even if you don't join the chamber, you can mine their site for potential contacts. To find a chamber in your area go to www.uschamber.com.

Rotary Club

According to Rotary International, Rotary Clubs are in place to "provide humanitarian service, encourage high ethical standards in all vocations, and help build goodwill and peace in the world." If you have a desire to help out those less fortunate than you, this may be an organization your business can participate in to meet other like-minded people. Just remember, this organization is not about helping you find business it is about helping others, but the relationships you build could lead to potential clients. To find a Rotary Club in your area log on to www.rotary.org.

Volunteer Organizations

Another place to meet people with similar interests whom you could build relationships with is through volunteer organizations. No matter what cause you are passionate about, there is an organization looking for volunteers. If you are passionate about helping end homelessness, volunteer to build a house with Habitat for Humanity, or if you want to help women rebuild their lives after leaving abusive relationships, volunteer at a local women's shelter. If you are passionate about animals, use your time to help out a local animal shelter.

Besides giving your time to volunteer organizations, you could also provide your expertise by giving them your products or services as gifts. For example, if you are an accountant, volunteer to help the organization with their yearly audit or serve on their board of directors as a financial consultant. If you sell beauty products, ask if you could provide a makeover for the women recovering in the shelter. If your home-based business sells gourmet dog food, ask the local animal shelter if you can provide them some food to send home with each new adoption. You are not looking for a direct sale, but people involved with the organization will see how much you care about the cause for which they are also passionate.

<u>Lists</u>

Buying a list is being mentioned last when discussing how to find potential clients because you will have no personal or professional connection with the person on the other end of the phone, letter, newsletter, or e-mail, and your marketing message has a high probability of falling on deaf ears or winding up in the trash. Should you choose to take this route, though, there are many places to obtain lists.

Listing Companies

There are numerous companies whose primary function is to compile and sell lists in just about every category and demographic imaginable. The company periodically checks, to the best of their ability, to ensure the lists are accurate. Buying lists is a relatively expensive and difficult way to find potential customers. National companies, such as Hoover's, allow you to pay a subscription fee and then search the businesses listed in their databases as often as you like within your subscription period. If you want a local list or list of residential addresses, check your local phone book for listing companies in your area, normally they are under the category Direct Mailing Businesses.

Phone Book

Speaking of the phone book, you can use it, as well as the online directories mentioned before, Yellow Book and Dex, to find business and personal listings. The print versions are only updated on a yearly basis, though. If you are worried about missing out on new listings, a safer bet is to use the online versions. You can then copy the contact information and put it in a spreadsheet to track your potential clients. There is a listing of more online phone book websites in the Appendix.

Assessor's Office

Another great way to create a list on your own for free or for a very low cost is to use an assessor's office. The assessor in your area keeps track of all property owners, including their contact information. If there is a certain zip code you are targeting, this is a great way to find everyone in a particular geographic location.

Business Licenses

If you are targeting businesses that may not be members of your local chamber of commerce, your local rotary club, or other professional organizations, check with your local government office for a list of business licenses. Some municipalities do not require business licenses for home-based businesses, but most require it for anyone with a storefront. The business license would include contact information, which you can use to determine a business owner's level of interest in doing business with your company.

Incorporation Listings

Another list resource is your state office for business incorporation. Where the information is gathered varies from state to state, but each business owner should file incorporation papers or at the very least, if they are a sole proprietor, reserve their business name with the state. These business name reservation and incorporation papers list the person or committee responsible for the business and corresponding contact information. Most states display them online, so it is easy to research these databases.

No Call List

Heed these words of caution: if your home-based business is calling strangers at home, make sure they are not on the National Do Not Call Registry, or the "no call" list. If you are soliciting people at home to sell your products or services to, your business must register with state and federal Do Not Call Registries. Your business could face severe fines if you call people registered on this list.

Being Successful in Your Target Market

Once you have decided on your target market, done your research, formed the picture of your ideal client, and located where to find potential customers, do not go chasing after other markets because doing so will weaken your company. Trying to be all things to all people is a recipe for disaster in running your business, just as it is in trying to make your products or services appeal to everyone. As a home-based business owner, you will need to either turn down work because it does not fit within your niche or you will need to partner with others who can do what you can't, so you can cover more ground within your specialty.

Be a specialist within your target market. By being the best option for your ideal client you will be the one that people turn to for those specialty products or services you offer. How do you become the go-to person for your target market? Be focused on what you offer and who you offer it to. It is okay to turn down work or pass a client on to a business partner if they do not fit into your vision of an ideal client.

Final Thoughts

It is your home-based business, give yourself permission to run it the way you want to. As the boss, you can work with whomever you want. To compete as well as be successful in your target market, you must clearly define who you work with and who you do not work with. Doing so will save you time and money. Use the questions in this chapter to define your ideal client and aim for your marketing bull's-eye every day.

5 DEFINING THE COMPETITION

Wouldn't running a business be great if you didn't have any competition? There would be no need for marketing. You would have a monopoly on the marketplace, and people would have to use your products or services. Unless you find a niche that no one else' has scratched, though, this is an unlikely scenario. Even as a home-based business owner on a shoestring budget, you can find out what your competition is doing with a little sweat equity.

Researching your competition is similar to defining your ideal client and your target market, only instead of figuring out what they want, you are figuring out what they do well and what they do poorly. Every business has something they don't do as well as the next, so if you can find that weakness and exploit it, you will be ahead in the game.

S.W.O.T. the Competition

You have already analyzed the strengths, weaknesses, opportunities, and threats of your business, now do the same for your competition. These exercises are not necessary for every company offering products or services similar to yours, but study some companies that closely resemble your home-based business or that you hope to have your home-based business look like. It is not wise to copy any business exactly, even if they are successful, because they may be stronger or weaker in other areas that you are unaware of.

Don't Be Scared

Don't be scared to do market research on your competition just because you might consider it too scientific. Getting to know your competition is like getting to know a prospective friend. It seems much less daunting when you think of researching your competition as a way of finding out what someone you may want to be friends with does for a living and how they do it. As a home-based business owner on a small budget, you should look at low-cost research methods and tools, preferably ones which won't take a significant amount of time.

Questions

Some questions to help you define your competition include:

Did a live person answer the phone?

When I did speak with a live person, what was the customer service like?

If they couldn't help me, did they direct me to someone who could?

What was the response time on my voicemail?

What was the response time on my e-mail request for information?

Did they provide marketing materials and a pricing sheet?

How do their prices compare to mine?

Do all their marketing materials, including their online tools, send the same marketing message?

Do they offer any special or unique products or services?

What is their online presence? Was I able to find them on all major search engines?

What are they doing for media outreach--do they have an online media page, send out regular press releases, or write articles?

How often are they in trade journals, in newspapers, or on television?

Do they teach seminars, online classes, or have speaking engagements?

Do they advertise? Where and how often?

Will they provide references and contact information for past clients?

What is their mission statement?

Do they provide their business goals and objectives in their marketing materials? If so, what makes them similar or different from mine?

These are just a few questions to get you started. Write down any additional questions you may have about your competition, especially ones that are unique to your industry. Where exactly can the answers to these questions be found? Read on and find out.

Research Tools

Once again, the methods used in finding answers for your target market are similar to the ones used in researching your competition. Start your search at the local library. Request that the librarian help you research other businesses in your industry that are similar in size. Find out the success rate of businesses in your industry, how many offer similar products or services, and what prices they charge. While this might be more information than librarians have at their fingertips, get as much information as you can from the library, then, once again, turn to the Internet.

Internet

If the librarian or other resources led you to the specific business names of your competition, head to the Internet and find their websites. Look up their business names on the major search engines, such as Google, Bing, Yahoo, and Lycos. Just by typing the business's names into the search engine you can get a wealth of information on them. You can find the answers to all the questions above by perusing their website as well as miscellaneous webpages linked to them.

Better Business Bureau

You can also find out about your competition from the Better Business Bureau. First, determine whether the companies you are focusing on are members. If they are, do they have good standings? Have they had any complaints registered against them, and were the companies willing to resolve those complaints? This will give you a glimpse into their approach to customer service. Most people are willing to switch companies for the promise of better care.

Chamber of Commerce

Your local chamber of commerce can also help you research your competition. They will more than likely have an online database of current members, often separated by types of business. Again, not only can you research your competition and target potential customers, but you can research other businesses through your local chamber of commerce.

Government Resources

As you did for the process of narrowing your target market, you can use free government information to research your competition. As mentioned in Chapter Four, government data is free of any copyright, so all information on your competition is public. The sites of the Census Bureau, the Small Business Administration, the U.S. Federal Statistics, and the U.S. Department of Commerce will provide you with business trends in the marketplace. (A full list of useful links can be found in the Appendix.) By knowing trends in your business niche, you will know how to best fit your products or services and business model within it. Government resources will not only provide you with current trends, but will also point you to changes in government programs that could potentially change the market.

For instance, when there is a downturn in the economy the government may provide more money for small business startup ventures. By knowing that, if your home-based business targets startup businesses, then you will have information on how to help a potential client that your competition may not.

Telephone

By actually talking to your competition, you can find out a lot of information about them just by observing the way they handle a request for information by phone call. Some industries, even when dealing with real customers, won't share their pricing structures or unique offerings up front because the competition is so tight, so while you might not get all the data you want, get as much as you can and develop a profile on your competition based on the most accurate information you can obtain.

Using the same Internet phone databases as discussed before, contact businesses in the same field as your home-based business. Give your competition a call and ask the same questions a potential customer would. This is a fantastic way of discovering how they treat potential customers and what the business has to offer. Before calling think about what questions you might ask, such as:

What do you want to know about your competition? Their

pricing structure? The type of clients they work with? What they offer? How they work their marketing strategy? Why people buy from them? What they offer that you can't? What you offer that they can't or won't in the future?

If you leave a message and they don't get back to you, it can be an indication that they are either really busy and don't have time for more clients, in which case you could offer to be a resource for them (this is discussed in detail later in this chapter) or it could mean they are awful at customer service, in which case you have now found an area you could emphasize in your marketing literature. To find out which it is, call the business back after a while asking why they never got back to you. If they neglect you again, then it is probably the latter.

<u>Types of Data</u>

Now that you know where to find the data, what types of data are you looking for to give you insight on your competition? Types of data can include public information, such as their marketing collateral or press releases, or internal data, such as their annual reports. If you are feeling daring and it's a possibility, you can even talk to one of the business's old employees.

Other opportunities to learn about your competition can come in the form of classes, seminars, or speaking engagements. Whenever one of your competitors speaks in public in a nearby venue, attend the event. They probably won't talk about their upcoming products or services, but they probably will reveal how they are doing business and how it is helping them succeed. People normally don't speak publically unless they are offering something of value or a secret to their success.

Compiling Data

Research won't do you any good if it sits upon a shelf. So what do you do with the data once you have it? Use it to your advantage by compiling it and sorting the results. This may sound scientific, but it's not--okay, it is a little scientific, but you didn't need to ace statistics in school to put together a study on the competition. It is simply about putting together a spreadsheet with the results from the different research tools you used.

Spreadsheets

When you determine which questions you want answered about your competition, set up your spreadsheet with the list of questions on the right side and the list of predetermined answers on the top of the page. Then fill in each question for each category. If one of your questions is, "How long have your competitors been in business?" write this along the side, then place the possible answers, A. 0-2 years, B. 3-5 years, C. 6-8 years, or D. Over 9 years, along the top, and then input that data into your spreadsheet.

For questions that are in more of an interview format, a spreadsheet won't be useful. For these, have a question as the heading and follow it with all the different answers gathered during the research process. Some of the answers may be similar, so you can track them by putting similar comments together on the sheet. This will allow you to compare your data easily.

Analyzing the Data

Once all the data is compiled and sorted, it is time to start analyzing it. This means looking for trends in your competition. Using the example above, have all your competitors been in business for longer than 10 years? If this is the case, then as a new business in the industry, you would have an uphill battle selling your company as the most reliable, so it would be better to position yourself as being the innovative and fresh approach to the products or services you are selling.

As a home-based business owner, unless you are looking for a financial backer, you should do sketches of your competition, rather than full-blown studies. It is not necessary to know everything about your competitors, but it is important to get a general sense of where your competition is headed and whether you want to stay in the boat or jump ship and swim upstream. The beauty of research is that it allows you to figure out what you want to do before you are in the water.

File the Competition

Once all the information is gathered, keep a file folder on your competition. Review the information as often as you review your marketing strategy. When updating your marketing strategy also update your competition file if necessary. Take a quick look at competitors' websites. See if they are still in business and if anything has changed in regards to what they offer their client base.

Meet the Competition

A great way to find out more about the competition is by treating them to coffee or, if you are feeling really generous, a meal out. Most people who have been in business for a while and are relatively successful are willing to help people who are just starting out. This is a great opportunity to pick the brain of someone who has been through the trenches and has come out in one piece, hopefully with their sense of humor still intact.

If you cannot find anyone local willing to meet with you or if you are a little intimated at the thought of courting the competition, there is a wide range of online communities supportive of people who are just starting out. Though finding a cooperative online community can be a little daunting, a great place to start is in the LinkenIn online groups, where there is bound to be a group to suit your business. Before posting a question, sit on the sidelines and observe the tone of the community. Some communities are incredibly helpful, while others focus on debates that often get heated. When you do find a community you like and feel comfortable in, throw your competition some questions. Some online communities will even provide you with sample contracts, agreements, or even pricing structures that its members use in their lines of work.

Partner with Your Competition

A great way to market your business is by partnering with your competition. Why would you want to partner with your competition? Because as discussed in Chapter Four, once you define your target market, you will come across jobs from those who don't fit your ideal client profile. It cannot be emphasized enough how important it is to be perfectly clear about what your business does and why.

So what does this have to do with partnering with your competition? Imagine you own an IT company specializing in helping homeowners with electronics and you get a call from a friend of a friend who heard you did IT work, asking if you would be interested in networking his small company's 10 computers. Now, you could accept this job, knowing you would spend just as much time researching the job as you would doing it because it is not within your specialty. Or, if you know of another IT company specializing in that exact service, you can contact them on your friend's behalf. Not only would you create goodwill with your competition by passing on their ideal client, but you could also ask for a finder's fee for your efforts. In return, your competition may pass clients on to you in exchange for a small finder's fee as well.

There is another way to team with your competition. If you have found someone successful in your line of work that has already shown a willingness to meet with you to answer your questions, you may also approach them for a mentoring relationship. A business with an established reputation has been marketing their wares for years and should have more business coming their way than they want to take on or can handle at any given time. So, by partnering with them, you are first in line for their business. Though you may be getting their castoffs, it is a great way to establish your business. A few words of caution, though: Before you partner with anyone, make sure to check out their reputation and standing in the business community. The last thing you want to do is hitch your wagon to a falling star.

Competing with the Big Dogs

As a home-based business owner, you may be scared to compete with larger companies because you may think potential clients won't want to work with a smaller company. Throw this idea out the window. You might not have the same financial resources as large corporations, but you have advantages, such as convenience, time, and money, to offer potential customers that your large competition could only dream of offering.

First, when your client calls your office, they are immediately put in touch with the person in charge of everything. You are the chief executive officer and the project manager. There is no hierarchy to go through before a decision is reached because you are the decision maker. As the saying goes, the buck stops with you. This makes the project more convenient for them.

Second, by working with only you, the customer saves time. Saving time is a great selling point because by the time the majority of large businesses make a decision and gets all the approvals necessary, the client could have purchased the product from another company or finished the project already. Because you are the only one responsible for their account, you can make things happen quickly.

Third, you can save the larger companies more money than other large companies can. As a home-based business owner, you do not have the overhead of other storefront businesses. This allows you to bid the product or project at a lower rate than your bigger competitors. Also, a corporation needs a job done on a long-term, but limited basis, it is cheaper for them to hire an outside vendor than to hire an employee that they may have to let go at the end of a project. Employees also come with human-resources costs, while, by working with you, they only have to pay your one-time cost. Companies want the most effective and least expensive option.

Final Thoughts

A word of warning about researching your competition, don't become so consumed doing so that you stop marketing your own business. It is possible to become so intimidated with what your competition has already accomplished that you consider giving up before even starting. Remember, even your competition had to start someplace and you have the advantage of following in their footsteps. They have made your business's entry into the market easier. You can learn from their mistakes, especially if they are willing to share their experiences through a mentoring relationship.

In the age of technology there is no reason not to research your competition. Target the business your ideal clients turn to on a regular basis and beat them at their own game using the methods described in this chapter. Whatever method you use to find out what your competition is up to, make sure to use it to your advantage and to not allow your research to sit on a shelf to collect dust. Do not allow yourself to be intimidated out of the game.

6 IMAGE AND DESIGN

Many home-based business owners are so excited about starting their businesses that they create marketing materials right away. This can result in materials that are cheap and easy to reproduce. While it is vital to stay within your marketing budget, if created correctly, just the image of your marketing materials can bring people to your company.

To start defining or refining your image, ask yourself these questions, "Does my image match what I envision my company to be? Does my image speak to me as well as to my potential clients?" This is where the description of your business and the place in the market you want to take plays out in your marketing collateral. In Chapter Four, you defined what your ideal client looks like; design your marketing materials around that definition.

Using Design

Use the design of your marketing materials to

communicate the benefits of your products or services. A key to closing a sale is answering any objections that arise in the mind of your potential customer. Having a design that expresses your message before you even talk to your potential client will reduce the amount of sales work you have to do once you meet with them.

Branding

The hip term to describe your image is *branding*. Branding has been around for as long as people were bartering and selling their goods or services. Artists in ancient times used symbols on the bottoms of their pots to identify their work. They were essentially the logos for their businesses. Value was placed on the pots based on the quality of the work and the artist's symbol on the bottom. Even today the value of your home-based business can depend on your choice of logos, colors, and style since most people remember image more than they remember what you have say.

Your business card, proposals, voicemail, website, letterhead, invoices, and envelopes are all identifying your company to your prospective and current clients. Branding your business has multiple benefits. Not only will your company become more recognizable and well known, but by displaying the right image, you can reduce questions about your company before they even arise. Though it is a good idea to have your business name cover what you do, sometimes we hear the name of a business and have no idea what it does. But the graphics and design along with the name often make all the difference in the world, and we are able to figure it out. Color and design are universal languages. They communicate tone and thoughts and create responses that your business name and tagline cannot.

The Meaning of Color

Though it is a big part of it, marketing is not just about number crunching and making a certain number of touches to an ideal customer to make the sale. Marketing is also about reaching your client emotionally. This is done through the use of color. Different colors have different meanings. Your image can communicate trust, humor, fun, or even environmental friendliness just by the colors you choose to represent your home-based business. It is widely agreed upon by psychologists and numerous studies have shown that the following colors have these connotations:

Red

Reds increase blood pressure, pulse rate, heartbeat, and even appetite. It is a high arousal color, and it immediately grabs people's attentions. This is the reason red is chosen in restaurant décor and for demanding attention in advertising, such as emphasizing the word "free" or some other call to action. It sends a message of energy, power, confidence, determination, love, and passion. Think of the red power tie in business or the red carpet rolled out at celebrity events.

Pink

While red is intense, its close relative pink is seen as soft and feminine. Pink is associated with friendliness, compassion, playfulness, and faithfulness. Pink is widely used for women's causes, such as breast cancer awareness, but it can also be seen as a weaker color, possibly because it is associated as being a softer version of red. For example, when someone is fired, they are issued a pink slip.

Yellow

Yellow represents warmth because of its association with the sun. Many day-care centers use it in their logos, often accompanying it with the sun, because it is seen as being cheerful, optimistic, playful, and enthusiastic. But, like pink, it has a dual connotation. When someone is considered a coward or weak, they are called yellow. Yellow is best used as an accent color, as it can be too intense to stand alone and too difficult to read in a digital format.

Orange

Orange, like red, is a very high arousal color and signals happiness, courage, optimism, and independence. Orange can work as a wonderful accent color in your designs, but could be overwhelming as the primary color choice.

Gold

Gold is seen as the ultimate in success. As witnessed every four years in the Olympics, where winning the gold medal means you're the best in the world, gold represents the pinnacle of performance.

Gold also symbolizes prosperity, elegance, and supreme

quality. Many businesses have what they call "gold standard service." An elegant way of incorporating gold into a design is through the gold embossing of business cards, stationary, and proposal cover sheets.

Silver

Silver is ornamental. It signifies serenity and purity, and is a classic choice. It also symbols money because the coin currency in America, except for pennies and other special issue pieces, is silver. As with gold, using silver as an accent with embossing will give an elegant, but modern feel to your marketing collateral.

Blue

Blue soothes because of its strong association with sky and sea. These elements in our environment are perceived as constant forces. Blue signals tranquility and intuitiveness, and conveys authority, truthfulness, and trustworthiness. Blue is one of the most used colors by businesses. Many banks and financial service institutions use blue to represent them.

Green

Green offers the widest variety of choices. It is strongly associated with nature, and not only sends a message of balance, healing, peace, and renewal, but also signals growth, abundance, and vitality because American paper currency is green. Since it has so many meanings, this color has wide design applications for companies offering natural healing remedies, organic products, business services, and once again, financial services.

Purple

Purple sends the message of being visionary, elegant, wise, romantic, and spiritual. It is normally preferred by creative businesses as the main color choice in their designs. Purple also has a sense of nobility and authority associated with it. It is also related to courage. For example, soldiers wounded in battle are awarded the Purple Heart.

Brown

Brown is associated with the ground and is seen as earthy. It conveys a sense of warmth, comfort, reliability, and stability. United Parcel Service (UPS), the shipping company, presents their marketing messages with their company color, brown, and the question, "What can brown do for you?"

White

White is seen as a symbol of purity, innocence, honor, and wholesomeness. Brides wear white on their wedding days and the packaging of many baby products is white. White is an eye-catching color when contrasted with dark colors. For example, an advertisement may be all black with just the call to action and the company name in white. White will make the message pop from the page.

Black

Black is viewed as mysterious, intriguing, elegant, and sophisticated. While some people associate black with death and mourning, the positive connotations outweigh the negative. When people think of an expensive event, they probably think "black-tie" and of arrivals in black limos. Also, when attending important business meetings, most people put on black suits. When they get married or attend special occasions, men wear black tuxedos.

Color Saturation

Different saturations of color can change the message of your business. Darker colors signal something that is upscale, rich, refined, and expensive. They show authority and prestige. While lighter colors send the message of playfulness, happiness, cheerfulness, exhilaration, and childlikeness.

International Color Meanings

If your home-based business has an international reach, do your homework before choosing colors for your collateral materials. Across international boundaries, some colors can be offensive to your target market. For example, the color white in the United States is a symbol of purity, honor, and decency. While in Asian cultures, white is used on death shrouds and is the color of mourning. The same color, with a completely different meaning.

Color Combinations

All colors, whether they are light, dark, or of different shades, have meaning. There are entire books written on the meaning of color and on the effect color combinations have. This is just a small sampling of the main color choices used in the majority of businesses today. If you have a color chosen for your business that was not mentioned here, there is a list in the Appendix of books that cover just about every color of the rainbow. Keep in mind, if you are having your materials professionally printed, some unique colors cost more to produce.

Typography

Colors are not the only way to communicate through your image. Even the font you use conveys a marketing message. There are two styles of typography, serif and sans serif. Serif fonts have lines or curves at the end of their letter lines. Times New Roman is a serif font and is seen as sophisticated, old fashioned, and elegant. Serif fonts are generally used for print formats.

Sans serif fonts, such as Arial, are viewed as more modern, friendly, and elementary. This type of font is used more for headlines and electronic formats. Once again, which one you use depends on the image you want your home-based business to express. If you decide to use script fonts, often seen as more feminine, make sure they can be read easily.

Should you decide to use an uncommon font and don't know what meaning or connotations could be associated with it, try this exercise: Look at the font and describe why you like it and why it would appeal to your ideal customer. Would the typeface make you stop turning a page in a magazine, pick up the brochure, or stop surfing the Web to take a closer look? Why or why not? Is the type easy to read? Many people insist on a certain script type when designing their marketing collateral, only to realize once it is printed, it is very difficult to read and their potential clients are not taking the time to figure their marketing message out.

Finally, when laying out your webpage, brochure, flyer, or anything with different font sizes, keep the variety in font types and sizes to a minimum so the document doesn't look scattered and confusing. A lot of variation will make your marketing message difficult to read, and your prospective clients will tune out the message you are trying to send.

Design Pointers

As has been touched on previously, make your image and design appealing to your ideal client. Knowing the preferences of your target market will increase the probability of success, but there are some basic principles of design, such as balance, image consistency, proportion, alignment, emphasis, unity, and simplicity, that are universal.

Balance

Remember playing on a teeter-totter as a kid? When both kids were similar in size, things were great because everything was in balance. But the moment one kid left or a kid of a significantly different size got on, things were out of balance. The same applies to your design layout. Unless balance is disregarded in a conscious decision to create tension in a piece, keep balance in mind when designing your marketing materials. This means not overloading the viewer with any one element of the design, such as text or graphics.

Image Consistency

Examine the consistency of your marketing materials.

This means making sure everything coming out of your office has the same message and image. The pieces do not have to be carbon copies of each other, but they need to be similar in tone and design. Lay out all your marketing collateral, including your online materials, and examine them. Are they similar in color, design, and character? If not, determine which image best suits your target market and use that theme throughout your materials.

Proportion

Proportion is how the elements in your marketing collateral relate to one another in size and scale. For example, smaller elements in the layout will recede in the background, while larger elements will seem to jump off the page. If you want a certain graphic, such as an image with a special offer, to grab your viewer's attention, make it larger than any other graphic.

Alignment

In kindergarten, most teachers graded coloring assignments on whether or not you could stay within the lines of the picture. While there are no predetermined lines for you to stay within for your marketing collateral, use alignment to organize your text and graphics in the layout. Alignment can mean having all the elements centered or in columns to create a synergistic look. Make each element flow with the next.

Emphasis

The emphasis, otherwise known as the focal point, is where you want to draw the attention of your ideal client to. It is the most important part of your message. Think of it as the bull's-eye of your layout. An instance of emphasizing your focal point would be creating text or graphics that stand out with size or color and leads your viewer to the call of action.

Unity

Having a united front is not just a good plan in parenting; it is also great for the layout of your design. Think of unity as the linking of two objects that while they belong to the whole piece, need to relate to each other. Unity is how well the parts work together to create a harmonious piece. For example, when using graphics alongside your text, have the text incorporate the graphic not only through words, but through placement. A graphic should relate to the story you are creating about your home-based business.

Simplicity

When people begin designing their marketing pieces, sometimes they are so excited about their products or services they want to tell or show everything at once. In design, this is a recipe for disaster. Sometimes less is more. When not enough white space or open area is left on a page, it creates tension and confusion in your viewer. Keeping your graphics simple and your text brief, while still making your point, will effectively keep your readers' attentions without making them strain to view your marketing message. Remember, white space is your friend.

Brainstorm Your Design

Before you lay out your brochure, flyer, website, or even

your business card, create a brainstorming sheet. Use this as the basis of all your collateral design. This is done by writing down your central marketing message in the center of a piece of paper, and then writing down what other messages you want to communicate in your design.

Set a timer for five minutes and use this session to write down as many ideas, phrases, or single words as you can about what you want your ideal client to know about your home-based business. At this point, don't censor any ideas. Just let your imagination run wild and tell yourself no message or design idea is crazy or can't be communicated.

Once the five minutes is up, look at all the ideas you have compiled. Now organize the ideas into themes. Some of your themes may be loyalty, trustworthiness, reliability, or innovation. Rank each theme on how important it is to your ideal client. For example, if you are in the financial services industry, one of the most important things to a potential client would be trustworthiness. Use these ideas and marketing messages as well as the design principles discussed above to assemble marketing collateral that will speak to your ideal client without them having read a word.

Types of Marketing Collateral

The use of color and design principles will make for outstanding office collateral, but what exactly will you be creating? Office collateral includes your logo, business cards, and letterhead, along with envelopes, brochures, pamphlets, flyers, and newsletters.

Logo

A logo is a symbol, sometimes accompanied by colors and words, that helps people identify your business. Simple is better when the logo is needed in multiple sizes. The business logo should be readable whether it is on a banner or on the corner of an envelope. It should also be readable in black and white as well as in color, and in print as well as in an electronic format.

A great example of a simple logo is Apple Computer's. There are no words associated with it, but no matter its color, their logo is distinct. The same is true for Nike's. When people see the swoosh they immediately associate it with the fitness giant. Coke uses their name along with their decorative type to distinguish their logo from that of their competition, Pepsi. The Pepsi Corporation now uses a red, white, and blue logo that is recognizable with or without the company name.

Business Cards

The design of your business cards also depends on the image you want your business to portray. With that in mind, business cards not only put your contact information in the hands of potential buyers, but they can be designed so your ideal client will hang on to them longer. In the age of technology where people input your contact information into a database then throw away your card, make people hang on to your card by giving them something of value. On the back of the card, you can have a checklist of things people need to do. For example, if you are a divorce attorney, offer a list of things people need to do immediately if they find themselves thinking about divorce. If you are a car detail business, have a checklist of what people need to do to keep their cars in great shape. If you have helpful how-to articles for your industry online, give link information on the back of your business card. People receive lots of business cards; make sure yours stands out by providing helpful tips.

Letterhead and Envelopes

When creating your letterhead and envelopes, it's critical to develop a design that looks great in print as well as in an electronic format. Make sure the layout design, which should include your logo and contact information, will work with your printer so you won't need special settings every time you want to send out a letter. White space is the biggest design element to consider when working on your letterhead and envelope designs.

Most businesses send correspondence through e-mail. When developing a proposal to be sent electronically, have your letterhead available in a word processing format so your proposal or contract looks professional. In any day-to-day e-mail correspondence, insert your logo along with your contact information into your signature line so you are continually building your brand with every click of the send button.

Brochures, Pamphlets, and Flyers

Brochures are the glossy, professionally printed marketing materials with professional graphics showcasing your strengths and what your home-based business has to offer. No matter how much money you put into them, though, most people won't hang on to a brochure. In this electronic age, unless you are selling high-ticket items, such as cars or expensive homes, brochures are an unnecessary expense when starting out. Most people want things electronically and as a home-based business owner on a limited marketing budget, your website design is your most important marketing brochure.

Pamphlets

Pamphlets are similar to brochures but present informative content, rather than promotional information, and they are not printed on glossy paper. Because of that, a great advantage of pamphlets is that they are cheap to produce. They can also be as big or as small as you want and can be easily sent out to potential clients by mail. Whether you are marketing products or services, pamphlets are a great way to not only showcase your strengths, but to provide something of value to your prospective clients so that your information has a longer shelf life. For example, if you run a landscaping business, your pamphlet could include five tips on how to make caring for your landscape easier. One of those five tips could be redesigning your yard so it is easier to maintain. Now that you have shown them that you can make their life easier, without high pressure sales tactics, your prospective clients have a reason to call.

Flyers

Flyers are another inexpensive option you can use to bring attention to your home-based business. When designing your flyer keep in mind that space is limited and that you must begin with your point of emphasis. What is most important for them to see? When a flyer is posted on a bulletin board or handed out at a meeting, you have a limited time to grab your prospective customer's attention. Try this test to see if your flyer sends the message you want. Ask someone who was not involved with creating the flyer to look at it for three seconds and look away. What do they remember most? What struck them as being important? Use their feedback to redesign your flyer so it sends the most effective marketing message.

<u>Newsletters</u>

Newsletters can come in either print format or in electronic format. This chapter will cover the print format, since more design principles are utilized in a print newsletter, while electronic newsletters, covered in Chapter Seven, are more often created from existing templates. Keep in mind that a print newsletter is costlier to create and distribute than one in an electronic format.

When developing a print newsletter, think about how often it will be going out, which customers or potential customers it will be sent to, how long you will you run it, and how long each newsletter will be. Will each newsletter have a theme? How much content can you generate about your industry? Before you launch your first newsletter, have at least six months of content mapped out. Determine whether you want your newsletter to be a marketing tool allowing people to see your expertise in your industry by providing informative content, or if you have a reputation already, whether it will be subscription based and become another source of revenue for your home-based business.

Whatever format your newsletter takes, provide useful information to your potential clients. If it is just a slick sales piece each time, you will quickly lose your credibility. What you would be creating each time is a marketing brochure? People do not want to read about how great your company is in a newsletter that was touted as informative and educational.

Trademarks

Once your logo is created and you are satisfied with the design along with what it communicates to your ideal client, consider getting it trademarked. Depending on the scope and reach of your business, you can decide to only register your logo with your state, or you can register it with the United States Patent and Trademark Office (USPTO). According to the USPTO, "a trademark is a word, phrase, symbol or design, or a combination of words, phrases, symbols or designs, that identifies and distinguishes the source of the goods of one party from those of others."

You don't have to register to claim the rights to your design as long as you can show a lawful use of the mark, but there are advantages to reserving the rights to your logo, tagline, slogans, or anything else that uniquely defines your business. According to the USPTO, the benefits of having trademarks are as follows:

"constructive notice to the public of the registrant's claim of ownership of the mark;

a legal presumption of the registrant's ownership of the mark and the registrant's exclusive right to use the mark nationwide on or in connection with the goods and/or services listed in the registration;

the ability to bring an action concerning the mark in federal court;

the use of the U.S. registration as a basis to obtain registration in foreign countries; and

the ability to file the U.S. registration with the U.S. Customs Service to prevent importation of infringing foreign goods."

If registering your trademark is a path you want to take to protect the distinctive aspects of your home-based business, consider talking to an attorney specializing in registering trademarks. For an inexpensive alternative, the USPTO has a great website (www.uspto.gov) that will walk you through how to research existing trademarks and how to register one on your own.

<u>Final Thoughts</u>

Making a sale more easily is what every business owner wants. Whether you are a born salesperson or a person with no sales skills, take the time to use color and design to your advantage. If you don't use them to your advantage, your competitors will.

7 MARKETING TOOLS

After identifying your goals and objectives, describing your products or services, defining your target market and creating an ideal customer profile, defining the competition, and creating your image and design, comes implementing the individual marketing tools you can utilize for business success. There is no magic bullet so using just one marketing tool to build your home-based business is futile: you must use several.

There are numerous ways to market your business: networking, using the Internet, creating promotional events, advertising, and cultivating media outreach to name a few. While some people say certain tools work while others are just not worth the time and effort, the home-business owner has a unique position. Normally, cash is in short supply, but sweat equity is readily available. So, for the purposes of this book, the discussion will focus on low-cost ways to get the word out about your company, even if they may take a little effort.

Networking

Before the opportunities of building your home-based business through networking are covered, there are certain practices that should be observed during networking functions and opportunities. There is a right way and a wrong way to network. The last thing you want is to be the person everyone avoids like the plague because of the scene created at the last business after-hours event. It is an uphill battle to recover the ground lost by making a bad impression.

By far, networking is the most important marketing tool for your home-based business. When the word networking is mentioned in most business circles, a groan erupts from the group and visions spring to mind of bad hors d'oeuvres, of people shoving business cards in your face, and of someone drinking too much of the free wine. After reading this book and finding out the proper way to present yourself and your business at a networking event, you will not be this person.

Networking Rule Number One

The first rule is to know what you want and do some prep work. Define a goal for the event. Whether it is to meet five new people, qualify three people to follow up with after the event, or gather 20 new business cards, have a set goal before heading off to the event. If possible, find out from the event organizers who are signed up to attend the meeting. Sometimes events are free-for-alls, but most organizations have at least some idea of who is attending before events start. If you get a list of names of people or businesses scheduled to attend, start doing your homework. Break out your search engine of choice, and get some facts on the businesses that you want to connect with at the event. Everyone likes to talk about themselves and hear about themselves, so if you can casually throw in a fact or two about their company, the representative will more than likely remember you and take your call when you follow up later.

Networking Rule Number Two

The second rule of networking is, don't try selling your products or services when you first meet someone. Nothing turns off a prospective client more than the image of a stereotypical used car salesman trying to figure out how to get you into this car today. When people ask what you do, by all means, give them your snappy 10-second elevator speech that covers how you can benefit them, or if not them, then someone they know. But do not try to close the deal right then and there at the event.

Networking Rule Number Three

The third rule is to have a great attitude. Be the first to smile, look someone in the eye, and have open body language. It is important at networking events to appear approachable. No one will talk to you if you are huddled around the buffet table or, worse, standing in a corner next to the fake vegetation with your arms crossed. Your body puts out more signals than your mouth ever could. Relax. Most people at networking events are scared or at the very least a little nervous to meet others.

Networking Rule Number Four

The fourth rule is to establish a connection with the person you are talking to. Try to find something you have in common. This is where the diverse background of most entrepreneurs comes in handy. Everyone has something in common and most people are willing to talk for at least a little while. If the person you are talking with is being difficult, give them a copy of this book with this section highlighted. Besides, if a prospective client is disgruntled at a networking event, where the whole point is to meet new people, imagine what they would be like to work with in the future. It is better to cut your losses and move on before you have sunk too much time into the relationship.

Networking Rule Number Five

The fifth rule will help you establish a connection with the person. It is important to have a mental list of questions to ask the people you meet. A few good examples are:

What does your company do?

Why did you start your business?

What made you decide to go out on your own?

Why do you like your job?

What made you come to this event?

If all else fails, break the ice by talking about the weather. No other topic is safer and more comfortable to people. Even people stuck in an elevator for a few minutes talk about the weather. Attempt to make the conversation flow naturally, but be thinking ahead to the next question you can ask when there is a lull in the conversation.

You get the idea. Essentially networking provides you the opportunity to ask almost any question that you are curious about regarding another person's business, within reason, of course. Don't ask if they use the same accounting practices as Enron, WorldCom, or Martha Stewart. Keep the conversation light, smile, make eye contact while asking your questions, and listen to their answers, which brings us to the sixth rule of networking.

<u>Networking Rule Number Six</u>

The sixth rule to becoming the ultimate networking guru is listen, listen some more, and then listen some more. Prospective clients will be immediately turned off if you ask them a question then look around the room and stare at the slice of cheese in your hand from the buffet table as they are taking the time to answer the question for you. Be genuinely interested in their answers. There is nothing worse than being asked a question only to be shushed because a bigger fish came along. Wait until the person is finished talking and then politely excuse yourself to make contact with another person. The same holds true if you are stuck with a person who bores you to death. When there is a lull in the conversation, excuse yourself nicely by saying you just saw another person you need to speak with or, as a last resort, that you have to go to the bathroom. Just do not make the person feel that you cannot stand to speak with them for another minute lest you fall over from boredom. You never know who that person may know or how you may need to connect with them in the future. Bill

Gates in his early 20s was probably not the best networking person in the crowd, so mind your p's and q's and you will be seen as the person to meet at an event. Also, by listening to a person, you might be able to connect them with another one of your clients.

Networking Rule Number Seven

The seventh rule of networking is to withhold your business cards. That's right, do not hand them out. This will not make sense to some people because business cards are one of the cheapest forms of marketing. The best way to make an impression with your business card, though, is to not hand it out to a prospective client until they ask for it. They are more likely to hang on to your card and enter it in their database if they specifically ask how to contact you in the future. On the flip side, if someone hands you a business card, do not just shove it in your pocket. Go to a networking event with a pen in hand. On the back of every business card you receive, write how you met them and note something you specifically talked about during the event, using shorthand or hieroglyphics if necessary. Doing this will keep that person fresh in your mind so you will not have to reestablish the connection at a later date.

Networking Rule Number Eight

The final rule of networking is to be you. This may sound simple, but then again, most marketing is simple. There is nothing worse than putting on a façade at a networking event and then having to keep it up afterwards. Do not try to be something you are not and do not represent your business as something it is not either. You will be found out. It is better to be up front and honest about yourself in the beginning than having to dig yourself out of a hole later on in the relationship. Once again, Enron, WorldCom, and Martha Stewart spring to mind. If you are concerned that people will not do business with you because you are new or home-based, then you do not want to do business with someone who thinks that way anyway. It may seem odd, but at networking events, you attract the type of people you want. By being yourself and representing your business honestly, you will get the most suited contacts out of the event.

Places to Network

The nice part about the business after-hours put on by your friendly neighborhood chamber of commerce is everyone knows why everyone else is there, so get into the fray, meet some people, and get some business cards.

Though your chambers of commerce are probably the longest running business organizations in your area, they are not the only organizations that put on events. Formal networking businesses, such as BNI, LeTip, and other small organizations, also known as leads groups, do too. The positive aspect of these organizations is that they only allow one profession per event. This means there is no direct competition in your group, so you have the corner on the market. The drawback is that some of these organizations are expensive and can quickly get more expensive if you are responsible for monthly dues or if you need to pay for the meal each time. Most of these organizations require you to bring in referrals on a weekly basis, so check their policy on if you are unable to bring referrals to the group, or ask other members. What are the consequences? Are you kicked out, fined, or mocked by other members of the group for the first five minutes of each meeting until you bring in more referrals? Check out each group before you sign up and attend at least one meeting or more before dropping down cold hard cash.

Some business networking events are set up like speed dating. You spend five minutes with each person at the event, get their information, and then move on to the next target. While this may or may not work in dating, use this method with caution while networking because it does not allow you to establish solid relationships with others at the event.

Other networking events abound, just check the business section of your local paper. Give the organizations a call to make sure they are still in operation and meeting at the places listed in the paper. Newspapers are notorious for not taking down networking listings once groups have disbanded.

If you do not find a networking group that fits your style, start your own. They are not that hard to organize and doing so will allow you to be in charge. This option is tough if you are new to your area, but other businesspeople are normally excited about the prospect of joining a new group of potential contacts.

Beyond the organized events, networking opportunities are everywhere. Some groups may even pay you or, at the very least, offer you a testimonial letter to network with them. "How can this be?" you ask. Consider volunteering your time to a nonprofit or another organization that you are passionate about serving. Whether it relates to golf, causes for children, cancer research, or writing, there is a board you can put your skills to work for. Serving on a volunteer board is a great way to meet people who will see what a charming, lovely person you are. They'll only be able to imagine how great it will be to do business with you. If you are not pleasant to be around, you may need to work on your people skills a little because networking is the best way to build your business.

An important component of serving on a committee is to be sincere. If you do not believe in the cause, though the organization would be a great resume builder, then find another outlet for your talents. People will see right through your motives, which could create enemies as well as a bad image for your company.

<u>Referral Building</u>

Getting referrals from your existing clients is the pinnacle of successful marketing because when people who have been told by their friends, associates, or family members about your great products or services call you, they are already sold. A word-of-mouth referral should be the easiest sale you ever make.

However, the million-dollar dilemma is how to get people talking about your business. The most important part of building a referral network is to ask. After providing great customer service, which is becoming extremely rare these days, you can ask your existing clients for referrals. When your clients start telling you how great you are and how much they enjoy working with you, it is time to send off a referral request letter. This is a document where you formally ask your existing clients to pass your name on to

other people who may need your products or services.
Two weeks after sending the letter, place a follow-up call
to your client. Ask them if they received it and if they
knew of anyone that you could help. Another way to
handle this is to enclose a prepaid post card or envelope
with the referral request letter, so previous clients can send
names back to you. While this is less scary for most
people, it has a lower rate of return than sending a letter
and following up with a phone call. An example of the
referral request letter can be found in the Appendix.

<u>Referral Partners</u>

Building your referral database is not just about getting
more business, it is also about working smarter. As a
home-based business owner, you'll find it nearly
impossible to cover all the bases a client might need
covered during the course of a project. Having a reserve of
businesses is a great way to streamline your process. It
means that you will not be scrambling at the last minute
against a deadline to find a resource to work with your
client.

Finding other businesses to collaborate with is relatively
easy. A great strategy is to locate other home-based
entrepreneurs who are looking for reciprocal partnerships.
For example, a graphic designer may look for a copywriter
to call on if the client does not have their own copy or if it
is so bad the designer would be embarrassed to put it on a
sales brochure. They may also partner with a computer
database administrator in case one of their clients has a
website that is database driven and needs coding done to
integrate the graphic designer's website.

In the section on networking, leads groups were briefly discussed, but these organizations' main goal is to share referrals, not only to build your customer database, but to assist you in outsourcing projects. Through leads groups you can meet other businesses to partner with on jobs. When teaming with another business or handing off one of your clients to work with another company on a portion of a project that you do not handle, make sure they live up to the same standards that your business adheres to. A surefire way to destroy a relationship with an existing client is to refer them to someone who will not treat them in the same manner you would. Investigate your referral partners' backgrounds and talk to some of their clients before recruiting them to help you out.

Voicemail

Your voicemail is an extension of your marketing message. Don't just use it to say that you are not available to take your customer's call. Use it to let callers know about upcoming products or services or about any special offers for that day, week, or month.

Party Time

Direct sales is a 29.55 billion-dollar-a-year industry according to the Direct Selling Association, so those selling directly to customers must be doing something right in their approaches to marketing. One of the key tools direct sellers use is the party approach. They invite people to an event--in their home, in someone else's home, or at an independent location, such as a meeting center, a conference room, or a community center. At this event, along with mingling, there is a presentation about a product or service. Consider using this marketing tool by hosting a dinner party or a wine and cheese party. This may seem like a tacky way to market your business, but there are hundreds of women who have used this approach and have a pink Cadillac from Mary Kay or white Mercedes from Arbonne International to show for it.

Contests/Sweepstakes

A fantastic marketing tool is offering a contest or a sweepstakes to create awareness about your products or services or to reward those who already use them. The prize for a contest or sweepstakes could include a sample of your products or services, tickets to a sporting event, or a gift certificate for a very desirable restaurant or spa. This marketing tool can be used as a follow-up to encounters at a trade show or at a presentation. At the event, ask potential customers if they'd like to receive your newsletter or tip sheet for the chance to win the sweepstakes or contest, and if they say yes, ask them to provide their name and contact information. You now have an instant list of new potential customers for your database.

If your contest or sweepstakes is big enough, you can include prizes by your referral partners and, in turn, make it even more attractive to potential customers. You might even consider approaching the local media and asking them to sponsor your contest or sweepstakes. The more impact your contest or sweepstakes has on another business or individual, the more appealing it will be to the media.

Gift Certificates

Offering gift certificates is a great way to market your business; you can use them in a couple of different ways. The first is letting your existing customers know about your gift certificate program, so they can buy gift certificates for the people they know who would enjoy your products or services, but who haven't taken the time or money to use your business.

The second way to promote your business with gift certificates is to donate them to worthy causes. The gift certificate could be for a fund-raising event or given as a door prize at a business luncheon. Some organizations will use your name, logo, and contact information in their promotional materials before and at the event, providing advertising that only costs you a donated gift certificate, which may or may not be redeemed after the event.

Bartering

When starting out or when you have little marketing dollars to spend, consider bartering your products or services for that of another business or person in your target market. You may offer a small product or a limited service in exchange for a testimonial you can use in marketing collateral, or if, for example, you are in need of printing services, consider approaching a small printing company--places like Kinko's don't need to barter--and offering something they need in exchange for getting your business cards or post cards printed.

A word of caution, get every trade in writing before you begin the bartering process. Feelings and relationships get hurt if expectations are not met in the way each person has in mind. You don't have to have a contract approved by attorneys, but at the very least have a letter of agreement drafted for all parties to sign.

Direct Mail

Direct mail is the process of sending information about your products or services through post cards, personal letters, or brochures straight to potential clients' mailboxes. Direct mail can be used after you have had initial contact with a person, as a way of introducing others to your business, or as a way of reminding them about what you have to offer.

Post Cards

Mailing post cards is a great, low-cost marketing tool to help you introduce potential customers to your business. Because people really don't have a choice about whether or not to open a post card, it is almost a guarantee they will read your marketing message.

Another way to use post cards is as a reminder to people about the benefits of using your products or services. By continually providing people with reasons to do business with you, once they are ready to move forward, your company will be in the forefront of their minds.

Depending on what you want to accomplish with your post card campaign, whether it is to get people to call you, sign up on your website, or attend a promotional event, design the post card so that you can track your results. Make it so people must use the post card to redeem the benefit you are offering. If you want people to call you or sign up on your website, provide a code they must enter to receive their first over the phone consultation or a special tip sheet. If you want people to attend your promotional event, offer free gifts at the event when people bring the post cards with them.

Letter of Introduction

When you meet someone who is interested in your products or services or when you receive the name of someone who may be interested from a mutual acquaintance, follow up with a phone call and a letter of introduction. The letter of introduction says how you met or heard about the potential customer and gives a brief overview of your business. The closing of the letter should include a date and time that you will call them unless you hear otherwise. A sample letter of introduction can be found in the Appendix.

Request for Testimonials

Asking for testimonials is in the same vein as asking people for referrals. If people are raving about the products or services you provided them, go ahead and ask for a testimonial letter. A recommendation from a real person or business speaks volumes of good things about you as a person and about your business. If the person wants to give you a glowing review, but is uncomfortable with how to write it, offer to write it for them and then get their approval before using it. Some people want to do it but are just so busy, it gets put on the bottom of their list. Once again you could offer to write it, but to make the deal a little more enticing, tell them you will provide a link to their site from the testimonial page on your website. Not only will this give them more publicity, but it will increase the ranking of your website because of the number of links within it. Testimonials should be included in all your marketing collateral; you could even put a quote or two on the back of your business card. A sample request for testimonial letter is included in the Appendix.

Word-of-Mouth Referral Request Letter

Develop a referral request letter for family, friends, associates, and networking contacts, sharing with them what your company does and requesting that if they know of someone who can use your products or services, to please let you know. The referral request letter is used with existing contacts and not as the initial point of contact. Include a prepaid postage card addressed to you in the referral request letter with blank lines for people to share the contact information of others who might be interested in your products or services. A sample referral request letter can be found in Chapter Eleven.

Sometimes getting people to share referrals is difficult because they don't want to impose on others, but to increase your odds, give people a reason to provide you with referrals. For example, if someone gives you the names of three people you can talk to, they receive free products or services.

Thank-You Notes

One of the most overlooked ways to market a home-based business is through writing thank-you notes. But doing so is a simple, low-cost way of setting yourself apart from the competition. Write thank-you notes to potential clients who listened to your presentation. If you met with a group of people, write a thank-you note to each person. A sample business thank-you note looks like this:

Opening:

Dear Scott,

Thank you for meeting with me yesterday. I know you are incredibly busy, so I appreciate you taking time out of your day.

Cover what follow-up will take place:

Please let me know if you have any questions about the information I left you.

I will be putting together a proposal for you.

I will call you next week with the details you requested.

Closing:

Once again, it was a pleasure meeting with you, and I look forward to working together.

Once again, it was a pleasure catching up with you. Please keep me in mind next time you need a new widget.

Sincerely,

Jane Smith

Sending thank-you notes is also a great way to let people in your community know what you do. If you receive exceptional customer service at the bakery, grocery store, shoe store, bank, or a department store, write a thank-you note to the employee as well as to the manager of the store. The handwritten thank-you note is becoming a thing of the past with e-mail and text messaging, so when people receive a note from you, with your business card enclosed, they will remember you and your company far better than they'll remember your competition.

A real estate agent didn't change anything in her marketing strategy, except that she started handwriting thank-you notes and thinking-of-you notes to people in her contact database. After a few months, she saw her business increase by 30 percent. She said it only took a few extra minutes a day, but the impact on her business was amazing.

Case Studies

In business, a case study is just a fancy term for a success story. A case study demonstrates how your products or services made a measurable impact on the life or business of a past client. When presenting a case study, you first describe the problem your client had. (Make sure to check with your client before divulging any information. You can offer to change the company name if they are hesitant.) Then you demonstrate how your products or services benefited them concretely by using such phrases as "a 75 percent increase in sales" or "a 90 percent reduction in wrinkles." The latter of which would be best presented with photographic evidence. Finally, close by saying how you could do the same for your potential client and providing one way your business could immediately impact them.

Sponsorship

Use sponsorship opportunities as a marketing tool for your home-based business. Most nonprofits need sponsors for everything from fund-raising parties to basic operations. Similar to using volunteering as a way to find ideal clients, find an organization you are passionate about and want to associate with your home-based business. Ask someone in charge if they have a sponsorship program. Find out what sort of participation is needed to get in their promotion materials, get a plaque on the wall, or be mentioned at a high-profile event. For example, if you are a party planner for kids, consider sponsoring a little league team. Your sponsorship may only be providing drinks and snacks at the end of games, but you will be in front of your target market a couple of nights a week.

Warm Calling

Cold calling is the act of calling a complete stranger in an attempt to set up a meeting, make a presentation, or make a sale. This is incredibly difficult and isn't an easy way to build your home-based business nor is it for the faint of heart. Warm calling is a different marketing tool altogether. It's when you call people you have already met, you have received referrals for, or whose companies you have done research on.

If you met someone at a networking event who fit your ideal client profile, the next step is placing a warm call to their office in hopes of setting up an appointment. If you were given their name by a mutual acquaintance, use the connection to help you reach your potential client. Have your friend introduce you or use their name when calling.

To transform a cold call into a warm call when you don't have a mutual connection, research the company before placing a call. Use a search engine or a business database, such as Hoover's, to find out as much information as possible and see if you do indeed have a connection. For example, if you are researching the CEO of a company you are trying to set up an appointment with, find out whether they serve on the board of directors for an organization of which you are a member. Use that as common ground when speaking with that CEO. A word of caution, do not lie about your interests or connections. Your integrity and reputation with a potential customer are worth more than anything else your home-based business has to offer.

Example of a Warm Call Script

Ask for your potential client by name. If you don't know the name of the exact person you want to speak with, when you call, ask for the name of the specific person who would handle the purchase of your products or services. Then call back at a later time when you can specifically ask for the person by name.

Jack Smith, please.

Use your potential client's name when saying hello. This will make the call personal.

Hi, Jack.

State your name, your company's name, and ask if your prospect has a minute to talk. You are trying to start the conversation out on a positive note, with a "yes." If they say "no," then ask when a better time to call back would be and set the appointment before you hang up the phone.

This is Bob Jones, with Creative Plants, calling. Do you have time to talk?

This is Bob Jones, with Creative Plants. Did I catch you at a good time?

This is Bob Jones, with Creative Plants. Do you have a minute?

Quickly summarize what you do by using your 10-second introduction.

I just wanted to ask for a few minutes of your time to briefly introduce myself and our company. We're a full service landscaping company that provides green ideas for people with purple thumbs.

Briefly tell them why you thought of them.

We had done some work in your neighborhood and noticed that the value of your home could be improved with a few landscaping changes.

Provide a quick testimonial story.

We've worked with many of your neighbors, and they have seen a significant increase in the value of their homes from our landscaping efforts. Sally Smith, four homes away from you, saw a 15 percent increase in the valuation of her home. I would love the opportunity to do the same for you.

Ask for the appointment.

I would appreciate 30 minutes of your time to meet with you and discuss how our landscaping service is an investment in the future enjoyment of your home. When are you available to meet?

When you follow up a second time--because you shouldn't stop with just one connection--say something like this:

This is Bob Jones. I contacted you on April 23rd concerning the benefits of using our landscaping services. I am calling to ensure you received my last voicemail message with my contact information. If you get voicemail, add: please give me a call at 212-555-5309.

Or if you sent them information they requested, change it to this:

This is Bob Jones. I contacted you on April 23rd concerning the benefits of using our landscaping services. I am calling to make sure you received the brochure you requested. If you get voicemail, add: please give me a call at 212-555-5309.

When placing a call, make sure you have an idea of what to say. For example, plan out answers to questions you think the person may ask. Do not just wing it. This will not work and it is impossible to make a second first impression. A script may sound rehearsed, but use it as a guideline if you get nervous and become at a loss for words. Also, smile when placing the phone call. Your voice will come across as enthusiastic. Whatever your script, keep your phone calls short and to the point. The last thing you want is to turn off a potential client by keeping them on the phone unnecessarily.

Should your ideal customer not need your products or services at the time you speak with them, ask if you can add them to your electronic newsletter list, then tell them it is educational in nature and very useful, or ask if you can follow up with them again at a later date.

Marketing Tools That Make Money

Believe it or not, some marketing tools will create a residual income as well as increase your staying power with clients.

Create a Workbook

Creating a workbook is a great way to have an alternative form of income as well as a great marketing tool for your home-based business. A workbook doesn't have to be complicated. You may already have the materials available; you just need to take the time to assemble them. For example, if you are a life coach and want to help people achieve their goals, you can develop a workbook where your clients fill out what their goals are, the steps they need to take to achieve them, and what their daily action plan will be to accomplish the goals in the time frame specified. If the person is really determined to succeed, they may hire you as a life couch to come alongside them and assist them in achieving those goals.

Develop a Program

The most important thing when developing a program is

to create or have something that only you can offer. This could be a new system for doing something in your industry or even a new way to sell your products or services. Even if you don't produce something new, you could develop a new way to package what you offer.

Developing a program consists of showing people how to do something on a simple and repeatable basis that gets results. For example, a personal trainer discovers a way to get into better shape in a shorter amount of time than usual just by the order and the structure of the exercise plan they developed. The personal trainer has clients who can attest to this fact, so the plan is developed into a program that can be used by anyone, as long as they have been cleared by their doctor for physical activity.

Another way to market your home-based business with a program while generating a stream of revenue is certifying other people to present or sell your program. Using the example above, if the exercise program is a success for everyone who follows it, the personal trainer will have more clients than they will have time to train, so they can instruct other personal trainers whom can teach their program. Each trainer will be required to pay a fee to learn the program, to pay an annual fee for teaching the program, and to attend update classes on the program. The personal trainer who created the program has not only created extensive word-of-mouth marketing for their home-based business, but they have also created a source of passive income.

Train Others in Your Industry

When you become successful in your business, a great

marketing tool you can use is teaching other professionals. Whether you are well-known for your financial success or for your abundance of knowledge, you can use your success as a way to help others in your industry along. Naturally, people want to know what steps you took to create your success so they can duplicate them. Offering training is a great way to market your business, not only through the possibility of finding referral partners, but through publicity you may receive from promoting your teaching seminars. Training others can also create another revenue stream if you charge an entrance fee or have your materials for sale at the back of the room where you hold the session. Send out a press release announcing every training session. Because they will see you are in a position to teach others about your success, the media may start calling you for expert advice on your products or services.

Attend Promotional Events

Whether you plan your own promotional event or participate in one that is already planned, attending promotional events is a great way to expand your database of potential clients. There are many options to choose from under the promotional event heading, such as trade shows, seminars, or speaking events. If you are not comfortable reaching out to people or speaking in public, these might not be the ideal marketing tools for your business, but try to get out of your comfort zone at least once and try one of these promotional events.

Before attending a promotional event, some of your other marketing tools should be in place. You should have your newly designed business cards, website, and programs to help you follow up with prospective clients. And if you are looking for future speaking events, you should also have a speaker's bio. A speaker's bio is a highlights version of your resume, where instead of offering bullet points of your accomplishments, you write out how your expertise and experience benefits the audience, normally in one page or less. A speaker's bio may be used by an event organizer to promote the event and could be printed in the take-home program at the event, so make sure your speaker's bio expresses your best skills.

Trade Shows

While taking part in a trade show may be cost prohibitive for some home-based business owners, it is an option for reaching a new target market. Before signing up for a trade show, though, get the complete details. Figure out the requirements, the cost of set-up and electricity, the sizes of available booths, whether anyone is allowed music, whether bringing food is allowed, and the available placement on the floor. The booths at the end of the aisles, at entrance points, and by the food are the best places to set up shop.

A marketing mistake businesses make at trade shows is expecting people to come to their booths while they just sit there. It is vital to get involved with the crowd. Have a way to draw people to your booth. It could be offering free samples that include your business's name and contact information or a giveaway to be awarded during or after the trade show. Above all else, make sure to have a system for capturing the potential clients' contact information. It could be having people enter a drawing for the giveaway prize or asking them to fill out a form to receive the larger giveaway items. An interesting option for engaging people with your booth is to have a trivia or computer game that they can play to win prizes. Before they receive the prize, make sure to have them provide you with their contact information. This is a great way to weed out the people who only attend trade shows for the free goodies; if attaining something requires some effort on their part, they are more likely to move on to an easy booth.

As in the jerky example from Chapter Three, where the vendor found more success at an outdoor sports trade show than at a specialty foods trade show, find a trade show where your business will appeal to the regular attendees but where you will be one of the few participants in your field.

Seminars

Running a seminar is a great way for you to be seen as the expert in your industry. A seminar is a forum where you share your knowledge with the audience. It can be held in front of a group of people or conducted over the phone in the form of a teleseminar. Teleseminars are less intimidating for most people and is a relatively low-cost way of hosting a seminar.

Provide the audience with practical, useful advice and they will love you. Give them handouts, whether they are copies of the PowerPoint presentation slides and samples of your products or services, and they will see the seminar as a valuable event and spread the word.

However, a seminar is not a place to make a sales pitch for

your products or services. When people think they are attending a seminar to learn something new, only to find out you are giving them a sales pitch and they need to buy something before they get anything useful, they become hostile. People are taking precious time out of their days to meet with you, do not abuse their trust by trying to sell them something. When you are open about sharing information, people will trust you and in turn feel more inclined to hire you or purchase your products.

One seminar held at a Small Business Development Center started out as an informational session, but as the two-hour seminar progressed, it became obvious that the company holding it was there to sell seats at their upcoming, all-day Saturday event. When attendees starting asking questions about the points the speaker was covering, the answer became, "We cover that in greater detail at our all-day seminar. Feel free to sign up at the end of the meeting." People were very upset by the end of the session. While the company may have sold seats to their Saturday seminar, they had burned a bridge with the Small Business Development Center and were never asked back to present again. Also, imagine how many potential clients they lost because they were shortsighted and only looked at the immediate goal of filling seats. Use a seminar to share your knowledge and potential customers will come looking to do business with you, instead of the other way around.

Speaking Events

Speaking events are similar to seminars except you do not organize them or carry the full load of the presentation.

Being a guest speaker at events is another option for raising the visibility of your business. You can be a lead-in speaker, a closing speaker, or the keynote speaker at an event. Once again, share your wisdom and your experience, along with a hopefully funny anecdote, and your audience will respect you for not wasting their time with a sales pitch. Imparting knowledge in an effective way is the key to building your business through speaking events.

To improve your speaking skills, you can join an organization, such as Toastmasters, whose sole purpose is to get you comfortable in front of an audience. The more you practice speaking about a wide range of topics, the better you will become at speaking to your target market.

The best part about trade shows, seminars, and speaking events is that they can become other streams of income for your business. While it is wonderful to pick up a client or two from these events, it is even better to get paid to speak and sell your collateral at the back of the room. Most people who speak publically about their success or their business earn more from back of the room sales than from receiving the speaking fee. So in addition to providing handouts, trinkets, and samples of your products or services, have items for sale, such as books, workbooks, or CDs and DVDs of past speaking engagements. You could even provide a signup sheet for people who want a recording of the event they just heard. Whenever you give a lecture, try to get it recorded. These days it is relatively inexpensive to tape an event, and selling at the back of the room is a wonderful way to build your business, with minimal effort.

Advertising

Advertising takes many different forms. It can be done through online magazines, websites, newspapers, Yellow Pages, radio, billboards, or television. As a home-based business owner, your marketing budget is limited, so it is critical to find advertising outlets that reach your target market. Advertising is the last thing discussed in this chapter because it is one of the most expensive ways to market your business and it takes many exposures, normally six, to get people to remember your home-based business. Advertising is much more effective if it has the right hook, if it has the right offer, and if it is used in conjunction with other marketing tools.

No matter what advertising you choose, remember the design principles discussed in Chapter Six and try to stand out from the crowd. If you are doing a black-and-white newspaper ad, instead of having black ink on a white background, do the opposite and watch your ad jump off the page compared to the others.

Once you have people looking at your ad, make sure your message says what it needs to at a glance. Every ad is trying to tell people something; what is yours trying to say? What is your ultimate objective with the ad? Is it getting people to visit your website, to call you, or to attend a promotional event? Your message won't be effective if you try to highlight all these things, so decide on what is most important for your business at the time you are running the ad and focus on that objective.

While large corporations can spend millions of dollars creating identity ads, you need your ad to produce results immediately. The only way it will get people to act is if it offers something they can't live without or that has a time limit associated with it, so determine what kind of promotion you want to offer. If you have one product or service in your arsenal that is hands down the most popular and keeps people coming back for more, make that product or service have a certain amount off or give it away free with the purchase of something else. When offering a discount on a certain product or service in an ad, use a dollar amount rather than a percentage off. People identify with firm numbers; it helps them quickly calculate the amount of money they will save.

Similar to the exercise with the flyer discussed in Chapter Five, have someone, who was not associated with the design of your ad, look at it for three seconds and then tell you what they saw. Did one thing stand out over another? Was the ad difficult to read? Did they receive the message you were trying to send? Whatever their response, use it to improve your ad before it goes to print.

<u>Final Thoughts</u>

Finding marketing tools that suit you and your home-based business is one of the keys to finding success. If you develop a marketing tool, only to have it sit on your desk or be too scared to implement it, time is being wasted. Choose marketing tools you're excited about developing and sharing with your ideal client. The best marketing tool is the sense of enthusiasm you bring to your presentation; that, above all else, will bring success to your home-based business.

8 INTERNET MARKETING

Internet marketing is not just about having a webpage or a blog; it is about creating an online presence. The first place most people will go to look up information on your company will be the Internet. If they do a search and nothing pops up, they may begin to wonder a few things. They could question whether your company is real or how long you have been in business. These doubts are very big hurdles you must overcome, possibly even before you start contacting potential clients. The first step to creating a storefront on the Internet is by creating your very own webpage.

Websites

In the business world, it's necessary to have a presence on the Internet. Having a webpage these days is about as important as having a business card. To be considered a legitimate business, you must have one. There are so many low-cost ways to build and host a website that there is no excuse for not having a presence on the Internet.

Whole books, really big ones, are written about designing websites, but here are a few pointers to get you started. Once again, keep in mind the image you want to portray. Going back to Chapter Two, if you are the Yugo of your industry, then it is permissible to use a simple site template from a company like www.GoDaddy.com, or setting up a blog on www.WordPress.com with a template design. But if you are the Volvo or the Bentley of your field, do not skimp on your website; make it one of a kind.

Before you begin developing your website, think about what is most important for people to know about your home-based business. Once again, this is where answering all those questions in the previous chapters comes in handy. When people first click on your site, what do you want their first impressions to be? If they go no further than your initial page, what do you want them to immediately know about you? That you have a special offer or that your hours of operation are longer than your competition's? What is your attention grabbing headline or hook that will make them look further? Determine what images and information will appeal most to your ideal client, and then have your website showcase that on the opening page.

What's in a Name?

Before you can begin designing your website, you need to reserve the name you want for your web address. It could be the name of your business, the initials of your business, the name of a product, or even your own name. The most important thing to remember when creating your web address is that it must be memorable and easy to remember. You can look up and register available names at websites such as www.Wordpress.com, www.GoDaddy.com, or www.Domain.com.

Designing Your Webpage

The design of a webpage is critical to success on the Internet. There are differences between your print media marketing materials and your webpage. They should all have the same theme, but your target market is not exploring your marketing collateral normally longer than a few minutes or even seconds. Your webpage, however, should make people want to grab a beverage, sit back, kick up their feet, and peruse your content. How do you make your ideal client do that? Through a few simple design tips, color choices, and great content.

Design Tips

Make your website easy to navigate. If you pick up nothing else from this section, remember this: do not make any information more than three clicks away from your homepage. This is as far as people will click to find the content they are looking for on an individual website. Yes, there are always exceptions to the rule, but unless your target market consists of bored people with difficulty sleeping, make your webpage as easy as possible to navigate by providing easy to read tabs as well as categories for the different products or services your home-based business offers.

Color Choices

Your website's colors should correlate to those of your

marketing collateral, but it's still important to note the colors you use specifically on your webpage because color plays an important part in how people will browse your site. While a red headline grabs attention in print media, red is difficult to read online and may cause eyestrain. Muted tones are best for your online storefront. So that your marketing collateral is uniform, choose colors that look good in print as well as in your online media from the beginning.

Flashing Your Clients

There is some debate about whether or not you should have a showy Flash presentation on your opening page, which once complete, takes people immediately to your homepage. While most web designers provide the option to skip the intro while the Flash presentation is playing, you must, once again, keep in mind the needs of your ideal client. Does your target market primarily consist of technically savvy people? Will your ideal client have the technology and the bandwidth to watch your video presentation quickly, or will it become so cumbersome for them to download that they will leave your webpage?

If your target market would gravitate towards a fancy intro, though, there are a few ways to optimize your marketing message through this presentation. Don't use the flash presentation to display your logo coming together or to create a nice picture with your business name on it. That will waste your ideal clients' time, which may lead them to believe there is nothing worthwhile beyond the Flash presentation.

Instead, use the Flash intro as a sales presentation. This

means using the video to showcase the unique talents and offerings of your home-based business in a short, concise way. For example, if you are a graphic designer, you can show different layouts, logos, or other design work you have done. If you are a public speaker or a corporate trainer, showcase your speaking ability by having a short clip of your best presentation. If you are selling products or services, use the presentation time to showcase photos of your bestselling items. However you handle your Flash intro, if you decide to include one at all, make it more than pretty--give your target market something to look forward to when they enter the rest of your website.

Essential Pages

There is a list of a few must-have pages for your website. Assuming you already have an idea about your colors and design after reading Chapter Six, make sure these pages are easy to read, not only through the verbiage, but through the color choices. Whether you are choosing a template web design or building one from scratch, your tabs should include your Homepage, your Products or Services page, your About Us page, your Media or Press page, and lastly, your Contact page, so when people are bowled over by your content they can contact you immediately to buy your offerings. Now that you know which pages are essential, you need to decide what sort of content should be on your website and how to make sure it fits within your company image.

There's No Place Like Home

The homepage is, by far, the most important page on your website. The content and design of this page help people decide whether or not they want to check out the rest of your site, or if they even want to do business with you. Your homepage has a tall order to fill, so look at ways to make it stand apart from every other webpage on the Internet.

Products or Services Page

Your Products or Services page showcases what you have to offer. Have the bestselling or most popular items on the top of the page so people do not have to scroll down to find what they are looking to buy.

About Us Page

The About Us page could be about you and your credentials for offering your products or services. For people who have been in business for a while, it could also contain the history of the home-based business. If possible, include why you started it. Potential customers will connect with you and your business when they know the personal side of it. It doesn't matter how long you have been in business, just why you started it. You could have started your company last month, but still have a compelling story about building a business around your passion.

Media or Press Page

Your Media or Press page is important not only because it allows the press to contact you, but because it shows your potential customers that you are a real business. Anyone can hang out a shingle on the Internet these days, but if they are not a legitimate business, the last thing they want is to draw the attention of the media. Like it or not, the television media carries a lot of credibility, and as discussed in Chapter Five, public relations is the one place where you are on the same playing field as the big companies. Remember, one television story can knock your home-based business idea out of the park.

Call Me

Arguably, the Contact page is the most important page in your web design arsenal (after the homepage), but the other pages make your potential customers want to contact you. Make your contact information easy to find and easy to read. Offer clients the option of calling you, e-mailing you, and sending you snail mail. Every person has a different preference for making initial contact, so give potential customers all the possible options to buy from you.

Choosing a Professional

If possible get your website designed by a professional whose work you like. Ask to speak with their previous clients to find out how well the web designer worked with them. While you want their expertise, they also need to be open to any input and suggestions you may have. The last thing you want is for your web design to be a reflection of the web designer's tastes, rather than a reflection of your business and the needs of clients.

Should your marketing budget not allow you to hire a web designer, at least get a professional's input on your site design before going live. It is almost impossible to overcome a first bad impression. Once again, you can get free reviews from Small Business Development Centers or in friendly online forums.

Register Your Webpage

There is no point in building a website if no one can find it, so it is important to register your site with all major search engines: Google, Bing, Yahoo, and Lycos. List as many related phrases and concepts as possible, along with your business name and your own name when filling in key words for search engine registration. Keep in mind how potential customers will search for you or your type of business. Remember, you will need to register every few months to keep your website near the top of search engine results.

Online Networking

You also have the option of networking online. Virtual communities abound on the Internet. No matter your target market, there is a forum for it. On the off chance you do not find a discussion group you like or that fits your criteria, you can create your own and then talk about it on other sites to bring attention to your community. LinkedIn, Twitter, and Facebook are a few great places to begin networking for your home-based business.

Blogs

Maintaining a blog is a great way to get your customers to see the real you and the real workings of your business, especially if being personable is part of the image you want to portray. As the old saying goes, people do business with people they like and know, not with slick salespeople. By opening up to your audience, they can relate to you on a personal level without you even being there.

A word of caution about using a blog as a marketing tool for your business: be careful about what you say and how you say it. You never know who could be reading your blog; it may even be your competition. Depending on how sensitive your industry is regarding trade secrets, you could open your company up to legal problems if you're not careful. Consult an attorney before you post anything that could be an infringement on another company's copyrighted or patented materials.

Message Boards and Discussion Groups

Participating in message boards and discussion groups is a great way to get free exposure for your home-based business. While these are not forums for blatant advertising, when you contribute to a group, you become a virtual member, and as the American Express saying goes, "Membership has its privileges." Why? When you provide advice, for free, no strings attached, people are given the chance to see what your products or services are worth. This may seem counterintuitive, but when you give a taste of what you offer after purchase, people will be left wanting more. It is the same concept behind the free food samples offered in grocery stores. If you try something you like, you are inclined to buy the whole package. Because there are people who abuse free samples, though, set your limits beforehand and realize it is okay to say "no" if someone is taking advantage of your advice. Besides people who are trying to suck the life out of your business are not the types of clients you want anyway. Another benefit of participating in message boards and discussion groups is that by offering your insight and showing people how your products or services can cure all that ails them, you will be seen as an expert in your field, which will put you and your business in demand.

Online Classifieds

Craigslist (www.craigslist.com) is a great online classifieds service. Started in 1999, this online community has local classified ads and forums for 450 cities worldwide. Currently, its sites receive five billion page views a month, making the chances high of someone who will need what you are selling seeing your ad. The best part about this site is that you can post what your business is offering for free, with the exception of job listings in seven cities and broker apartment listings in New York City. Yes, it is a place for free online advertising, a place to sell your wares without paying a fee for placement. So if for some reason your stuff does not sell, you are only out the time it took you to write the post, which you can run on every section of the Craigslist community, not just on the pages for your area.

There are other online markets that have free classifieds and advertising opportunities. Just remember what place you want in the market and have your message reflect your overall business image. For a list of more sites like this, see the Appendix.

Make Yourself an Internet Star

Whether it is for view as a podcast or on the most popular video download site, YouTube (www.YouTube.com), you can create an audio clip or a video positioning yourself as the expert in your niche market. This doesn't mean you should make a video of yourself burping the ABC's; this is a place for a presentation you created or will create specifically for posting on the Internet. Once again, make sure the media is professional and projects the image you want to create for your home-based business.

If you are creating a video from scratch, consider using a conference room to record it. No one else has to be in the room if you have a fear of speaking in front of people but have no problem putting yourself out in the digital world. A list of websites where you can upload your videos can be found in the Appendix.

<u>Electronic Newsletter</u>

With services like Constant Contact (www.constantcontact.com) or iContact (www.icontact.com), reaching your customers and potential customers on a regular basis through an online newsletter is easier than ever. These services have hundreds of templates already created, and at least one should be in the same style as your overall marketing image. You can also embed your logo in the template to further brand your business. Consider the same questions posed in Chapter Six about print newsletters before launching the online version.

When people read information on their computers, they have very short attention spans. Unlike a print newsletter, an online newsletter should be limited to one page and be written in a format that allows your readers to browse. This means creating easy to read headlines, creating bullet points of the most important themes, and writing in short paragraphs. Paragraphs should be limited to three or four sentences.

Continue to keep readers' interests by putting a few graphics in your online newsletter. Some pictures including people will help your customers identify with your newsletter. The type of people you display depends on the content of your newsletter. If you are discussing serious business topics, pictures showing people frolicking on the beach won't help readers relate to what your newsletter topic is covering, unless you're promoting a vacation package or a retirement plan.

Electronic Tip Sheet

If the thought of creating a newsletter on a regular basis feels overwhelming and time consuming, consider developing a tip sheet. This is an even shorter version of a newsletter and can just be a paragraph or simple bullet points briefly discussing a topic of interest in your industry. Remember, whether you create a newsletter or a tip sheet, make it helpful and educational to your readers or it could be viewed as spam.

Speaking of spam, and that is not a reference to the canned meat by Hormel, before sending people your online newsletter or tip sheet, make sure recipients have opted in through signing up on your webpage or in some other way, such as signing in at a presentation you gave. If you send your electronic newsletter repeatedly to people who don't want it, you could be blacklisted and, worse, you could lose potential customers.

If you are ever in need of content, there are sites where

you can download articles for free or for a small fee. The list in the Appendix concerning article submission sites can be accessed for content on just about every subject imaginable. Wherever you get your content from, though, unless you created it, abide by all copyright laws and laws concerning reprinting that are associated with the article.

E-zines

An e-zine is an online version of a print magazine. You can copy the format of a typical print magazine, with advertisers and different articles all under the umbrella of a similar theme for each issue, or you can design it specifically for the web. To keep startup costs low, you can omit advertising. It can be distributed as often as you like, and you will have no printing costs.

E-zines are a great way to create awareness about your industry. If your products or services need some explanation before sales are made, developing an e-zine for your target market might be the way to go. Newsletters should be limited to one page, but an e-zine can be as long as you want to make it. As discussed with newsletters, you can use other writers' content if you are at a loss for words, but an e-zine should be about the special benefits of the products you offer or about showcasing your talents and abilities in the services industry.

Developing an e-zine is relatively simple because of all the templates and list management systems available online. The beauty of creating an e-zine is that it can bring in an alternative stream of revenue for your business. Your e-zine could be set up in a couple of different formats to make you money with only a little effort.

First, you can sell advertising space like you would in a typical print magazine. While you don't want to create more work for yourself by calling on local businesses that have no interest in reaching your target market to advertise in the e-zine, you can approach other businesses in your industry or approach your referral partners. Your referral partners might be other businesses in your industry that have the same target market, but sell different products or services than you do. Again, a graphic designer could be a referral partner with a copywriter. The copywriter may want to advertise to the graphic designer's clients who need better content written for their marketing collateral, while the graphic designer will appeal to those seeking better content, but whose sites or marketing materials are not up to par.

The second way to generate money with an e-zine is to sell content space. You can approach the same referral partners you would about advertising to see if they are interested in contributing content to the e-zine. Charge a small fee for the privilege of accessing your clients through your e-zine. Selling content space takes a little longer to develop because you will have to show a database of readers before this is profitable for your referral partners. With applications such as Wordpress.com you already have a built in counter for the number of followers.

E-Books

E-books are another low-cost way to create credibility while providing a resource for people interested in your products or services. The largest book distributor in the world, Amazon.com, allows anyone to upload an e-book and download it to their Kindle on the same day. There are a few differences between an e-book and a printed book. The differences are cost, length, and profitability.

Cost

Although it is not as costly as it used to be, you still have to shell out money to create a print version of a book. An e-book primarily costs you time, and if you are just starting your home-based business, time is something you have a lot of, while money is sometimes scarce.

Length

An e-book can be incredibly short. Some e-books are no longer than a few pages, and two chapters may appear on one page when printed out. However, if you are planning on charging for your e-book, something a little longer and with a little more content will be in order.

Profitability

The best part of creating an e-book is the profitability potential. Though you will have invested your time into the e-book, there are minimal hard costs associated with it. Most people already have word processing programs on their computers, so while you might need to purchase software or pay someone to create a PDF of the document, which is about it for costs. Because it will be an e-book, your manuscript can be updated regularly to remain current with the trends in your industry, and you'll be able to resell the updated manuscript to your existing database of clients.

If you want the visibility of a book, but don't have the writing ability to pull it off, consider hiring a ghostwriter for your project. You can approach local colleges, post an ad to an online bulletin board, or use online classifieds to search for people interested in ghostwriting projects. A word of caution, though: most aspiring writers watch freelance writing listings like hawks and your inbox will be inundated with people willing to work with you. Think about setting up a separate e-mail account from Gmail, Hotmail, or Yahoo to deal with the volume. As with any service business dealing, ask to see work samples and testimonials from people who have used their writing services in the past.

E-books are also another way to link yourself with your referral partners. For instance, your referral partner wants to provide more downloads or content on their website. You can offer them your e-book and get paid for this contribution in a couple of different ways. The first option is selling the e-book for a one-time cost. The danger of this is you only receive a one-time payment, rather than a continual stream of income, but if your referral partner's website has the traffic you desire and a one-time payment is the only way they will take the e-book, you might want to consider this option. Another option is taking a percentage or a certain dollar amount for each book sold. If the book starts selling like hotcakes, this would be the most profitable way to go and a great way to generate clients for your business.

Webinars

Webinars are virtual seminars where you interact with the

attendees. It doesn't matter if you are marketing products or services; a webinar is a low-cost way to promote your expertise as well as the benefits you can offer potential customers. This forum is perfect if your ideal clients are located in different areas. Visual communication companies, such as WebEx (www.webex.com), can help you organize and promote your webinar.

Webcast

A similar online format is a webcast. Unlike using YouTube, which allows your videos to be found through searches, a webcast has a list of attendees who are invited to your presentation. And unlike webinars, webcast presentations are one-sided. You share the information, but your audience is unable to ask any questions. One of the benefits of hosting a webcast is that you can offer it as a download on your website so potential customers can see it over and over again.

Online Classes

If you want to share information with others in a classroom format, but are scared to death of teaching in front of people, you might want to consider teaching an online class. This medium allows you to share your knowledge over a period of time. Teaching classes is more applicable for those in the service industry. For example, if you are a writer and want to help people become better writers, you can teach several short courses on writing. The topics could include grammar basics, how to write fiction, how to write nonfiction, and how to write business correspondence.

Final Thoughts

The Internet is here to stay, so it is vital your home-based business have a place online. If you only use one marketing tool from this chapter, make sure it is the website. If you don't have one, your sales will go to your competition simply because they have online presences.

9 REACHING THE MEDIA

The media is everywhere these days, and it is constantly looking for stories. Thankfully, public relations are one of the few areas where the big companies and home-based businesses are on a pretty even playing field. The media loves an underdog, so stories where small businesses overcome giant obstacles to compete with big business hook them. The biggest complaint reporters have about public relations done by home-based business owners is that their stuff is not newsworthy. This chapter will help your home-based business become newsworthy.

Before you can become newsworthy, though, think about the overall media strategy of your business. Yes, once again, you need to put pen to paper or fingers to the keyboard. It only needs to be a page, if that, but you need to map out how your business will be interacting with the media. The following is a list of possible media tasks:

Map out a press release every month for a year. (Ideas for generating monthly press releases will be covered a little later.)

Plan out letters to the editor, and when and where they will be sent.

Send out query letters to media outlets.

Approach media outlets about writing specialty articles or advice columns.

<u>Press Kits</u>

While this might not be necessary for most home-based businesses right from the start, you should have a press kit ready after sending out a few press releases. A great way to handle press kits is on your website. Once you get some press coverage--these are called clips--post them on your website along with the material discussed below.

A press kit includes a biography about yourself and anyone else who may be involved with your business. The biography should cover your professional, not personal, life, unless your business is based on some deeply personal event in your past. Think of the biography as a beefed-up resume. Instead of bullet points about what you do in the company, it is a page or two about your life as it relates to your expertise in your field. This might be covered on the About Us section or under the Media tab of your webpage, but make sure it is easy for busy reporters to find.

Another element of the press kit is a professional photo, with emphasis on professional. Just because your business is home-based doesn't mean the picture should be of you in your bathrobe and bunny slippers. While many of you may be saying to yourselves, "Well, duh!" you may be surprised at how many pictures people put up on their websites that they deem as professional but that are not truly in accordance with the image they want their businesses to uphold or with the prices they are demanding.

Press kits should also include any other media coverage the business has received in the past. Include newspaper clippings, magazine clippings, and television appearances. If possible, have the print media clip written out on your website and provide a link to the page on the media website where it was originally posted. With television clips, if they are not already online, contact the news station covering the story and see if they could e-mail you a digital file or the electronic link so you can post it on your website. Most news stations want as many links as possible to their websites, so normally they are more than willing to supply this information.

Having a press kits is a great way of getting more media coverage from past media coverage. If reporters see you have experience working with the media, they are more likely to contact you for a story quote or tap into your expertise.

Press Releases

Writing press releases is an easy way to get your name in print and receive some publicity for your company. People in the media have a couple of little secrets they do not want you to know, but those secrets will be exposed here.

The Press Needs You

They need you just as much as you need them. In this 24/7 world, news is happening every minute of every day. Due to the demand of print, television, and online media outlets, reporters are always looking for good stories. Notice the word "good" – not great, not fantastic, and not controversial. Most people seem to think their home-based businesses have nothing to say that would intrigue the media. Get this thinking out of your head right now! Say it out loud, "I am newsworthy. I am newsworthy. I am newsworthy." If you need to say that a few more times to yourself, possibly in front of a mirror, go ahead, the rest of this section can wait.

Okay, you're back. Are you convinced that you and your home-based business are newsworthy? If not, here are a few examples of some top stories from the local news: "Dogs Have Wedding Ceremony After Meeting at the Local Dog Park," and "Do Breath Freshening Products Actually Make Your Breath Worse?" If that is what the local news producers view as important, then your business can get airtime too.

Make Your Press Releases Current

News about your business can be whatever you want to make it. You can even link your business to a calendar event. For example, January is National Organization Month. This can be used as a lead-in for a home-based professional organizing business. Websites like Earth Calendar (www.earthcalendar.net) let you know about a holiday for just about every day of the year. Align your products or services with a special day or month while stating why your business makes the holiday easier to handle, easier to work through, or less stressful, and send out the press release.

You can also make your press releases relevant to hot stories in the media. Tie them in with current events. Some of you are now thinking, "How is my business even remotely connected with the current events?" Here is an example of working off current events: the local business section of a newspaper stated that, currently, the biggest problem employers were having was compensating for their women employees being out on maternity leave. Employers were trying to figure out how to pick up the pace while these women were out. Since a solution was not formed in the article, a small business sent out a press release about the availability to hire expert consultants, not just for temporary help, but to fill these positions on a short-term basis while women were out on maternity leave. The press release was titled, "Novel Idea Gives Birth for New Way to Due Business." Within five minutes of sending the press release out, a call came in from a reporter about a follow-up story. He had not even read the whole press release when he called.

<u>Tantalizing Titles</u>

The next tip for creating a great press release is to create a catchy title. As you did for the mission statement of your marketing strategy, you should take a stab at a catchy title before writing the press release, but once the press release is completed and you are ready to send it out, you should work on the title again. Sometimes it is all the reporter will see before they hit the delete button.

While one title may be great for one publication, it may need to be changed for another. Here in lies the next rule of a great press release, know your audience. If the press release is about a grand opening celebration or a general interest topic, then you might only need to change the title for each publication. However, if you are launching a new service or product within your business, each press release's title should be framed to target the markets the press release is being sent to. For example, if your new product will help organize all the widgets in people's homes or in their offices, then the first press release sent to the local business journal would be titled, "Improve Your Bottom Line with Organization Widget." If your press release is sent to the home section of the newspaper, then it would be titled, "Improve Your Family Life with Organization Widget."

Keep It Short and Sweet

Make your press release short and simple. Press releases rivaling *War and Peace* in length are not likely to be printed. Do not make your press release about you and how great your company is. Reporters will smell an advertorial before they open your e-mail. Instead, make the press release about how your products or services will help the general public by saving them time, money, energy, or by fulfilling some other need. Go back and review the benefits of your products or services if you need to get your juices flowing.

Make It Human

Another element that catches reporters' attentions is the human side of a story. Reporters have said they want one of the following elements in a potential story: controversy or sweet and sappy. Since being featured on *20/20* as the latest scam in the world of business hopefully isn't one of the goals of your home-based business, focus on the sweet and sappy angle.

By working the sweet and sappy angle, you may not only get in the business section of the media, but in the human interest section as well. Keep thinking about the saying, people do business with people they like and trust. If your potential customer base sees you as someone who has overcome insurmountable odds to start their business or started their business because of those insurmountable odds, you already have a great story. If you don't have that kind of an experience, though, do not make up a story about how bad your life has been. It is better to keep the integrity of your business intact.

Grammar and Spell Check Count

The press release must be impeccably written and grammatically correct. If you do not have the ability to write effectively and do not want to learn, hire a copywriter, a public relations consultant, or an editor. Normally copywriters are less expensive than public relations consultants and write just as well if not better. If you do not have the budget to hire a copywriter, a public relations consultant, or an editor, find your nearest Small Business Development Center and ask if one of their consultants can meet with you to review your press release. While the Small Business Development Center consultants will not do the work for you, they should be willing to review your work and offer some suggestions. The best part is all of their help is free.

Sending It Out

Sending out the press release is the final step in the process. Assuming you do not have the budget to hire a public relations consultant to send out the press release, this is where you let your computer mouse do the clicking. The Appendix lists great sites to find contact information for the media in your area. Local television stations have webpages designed to make it easy for you to alert them to a news tip or submit your press release.

When sending the press release electronically, put it in the body of the e-mail. Reporters are just as scared of computer viruses as you are and will delete an e-mail with any attachment. This includes electronically attached business cards. In the subject line of the e-mail, put, for example, "Media Release: Bonzo's Costume Shop Is Not Just Clowning Around." This way, the recipient will know it is a legitimate e-mail.

Finally, send the press release out twice. Yes, send it out twice, approximately two weeks apart. The first e-mail may get lost or accidentally deleted, so if a media outlet has not picked up the press release, send it to them again. If they do not pick it up the second time, though, move on to another press release or publication.

There are sample press releases in Chapter Twelve.

Story Pitch

A story pitch is written so all the reporter has to do is interview you for a few missing details or have you appear on television to flesh the story out.

Most television stations have a list of reporters' contact information. News outlets have different reporters for different topics. Send your story pitch to the most suited reporter directly. Read or watch the media and find out who covers what. It is a waste of your time to send a business story to the education beat reporter just because you know her e-mail address. Take the time upfront to do a little homework and your success rate will increase dramatically.

Letters to the Editor

Sending letters to the editor is an effective way to let the media know you are available as a reference for future stories. There are two versions of a letter to the editor. The first is, when you see a story about your specialty in which the writer is a little off the mark, you can send a letter to the editor discussing, in a friendly way, where the writer could have improved the story. Close this type of letter to the editor by offering your expertise as a resource for future articles. When writers need real-life sources, sometimes they ask the editor if they have anyone in mind, so by doing this, you will be a step above sources out of the phone book.

The second version of a letter to the editor is one in which you offer your services as a resource for future articles. This is essentially a sales letter about your business that isn't too self-promoting. It is a delicate balance to attain, but you do not want to turn off the reporter before you get their attention. The letter should cover your business and what makes you the expert in your field. It might be the number of years you have been in the industry, a special way your products are designed, or how you handle your services. Emphasize what makes you different from others in the industry. Finally, tell the editor how accessible you are, that you are available even on short notice for a quote. Then be available. Do not start your letter writing campaign right before vacation time. Include the numerous ways the editor or his reporters can contact you.

In each version of the letter, include one or two copies of your business card for the editor to keep on file or to at least put into their electronic database. Once you have mailed out either version, follow up with the media outlet two weeks later to make sure they received the letter and to answer any questions they may have.

Examples of both of these versions are included in Chapter Twelve.

<u>Query Letters</u>

Sending a query letter is the equivalent of sending a story proposal to a media outlet. The nice thing about doing a query letter for your business is that if a publication likes it they will pay you to write for them. Before you go looking for a media outlet to send your story ideas to, though, there are a few basics to keep in mind. Some of these are common sense things, but they bear repeating to increase your rate of response.

<u>Contact the Right Person</u>

Address the query letter to the right editor and send it to them by mail, e-mail, or fax, whichever they prefer.

Databases, such as those of *Writer's Market* and Wooden Horse Publishing, will help you find contact information for publishers. You can pick up a copy of *Writer's Market* at your local library for free or pay a small fee for the online subscription. Wooden Horse Publishing is more expensive and should probably be reserved for a person who sees pitching to magazines as an integral part of their marketing plan. Call to verify the editor is still working at the publication once you do have a name. Some editors change jobs about as often as some people change their underwear, and it is difficult for large databases to keep track of all the shuffling.

More Hooks

The hook is meant to grab the editor's attention so they continue to read your story idea. You can develop a hook for a query letter using the same tactics for developing a press release hook. Tie your story idea into current events, government statistics, or a new development in your industry. If the query is a blatant attempt at self-promotion, then the story will not be picked up by the publication. An example of a hook that works is: "Whether your office is an hour from home, 30 seconds from your bedroom, or in your bedroom, clutter and disorganization impact your bottom line." Now the editor wants to know how clutter impacts the bottom line and what can be done to stop it. So she reads on and finds the next part of your query letter, which describes the article you are pitching.

This portion of the query letter lets the editor know what they can expect from the article. Continuing with the example above, the query letter included five steps to reducing clutter in the office. The standard length for query letters is no more than a page, but if you honestly believe that you need to give more information to the editor, and then do it.

Qualifications

The next component of a query letter is telling the editor why you alone are qualified to write the article. It may be your work experience, the type of products or services you sell, or even a personal experience with the story. Using the above example about organization in the office, the writer may be qualified because they are a professional organizer or have a product that helps anyone get organized.

Contact Me, Please

Probably the most important part of a query letter is your contact information. Many people think an editor will love a story so much they will search them out so the competition does not get a hold of the hot lead. While the story might be in demand, no editor is going to take time to Google you or your business to contact you. So at the end of the letter or e-mail, include all the different ways the publication can contact you. Make sure to include your website address.

Make It Perfect

Finally, proofread your query letter before sending it out. In this world of instant messaging and e-mail it is very easy to hit the send button and hope for the best. But a query letter will be deleted or tossed in the trash if it has too many misspellings or grammatical errors. However, do not obsess so long over your query letter that it becomes outdated. Just give it a read out loud before stuffing the envelope or hitting the send button.

A sample query letter is included in Chapter Twelve.

Sending Out the Query

Now that you have written an excellent query letter, where should you send it? The previously mentioned databases, *Writer's Market* and Wooden Horse Publishing, are a few resources, but there are other great, free online resources for you to use. The first is Trade Pub (www.TradePub.com), which is a listing of trade magazines. These are magazines specializing in specific industries and are normally looking for quality material that informs their readers about new trends in the market. Another option is Find Articles (www.FindArticles.com), which lets you search a collection of magazine articles. More websites are listed in the Appendix.

Specialty Articles

Developing a query letter and sending it off to publications in hopes of your story getting accepted can be a little daunting for home-based business owners who want simple and immediate results after having taken the time to write an article. This is where the beauty of specialty articles and the Internet comes into play. The Internet has opened up a whole new realm of opportunities for the home-based business owner to attain publicity through writing. A specialty article is an article that is written simply for publicity, not that this means a version of your marketing materials is sent out and called an article. Once again, the rule is to write an informative and educational piece.

The difference between developing a query letter for an article and writing the specialty article is that you normally will not get paid for a specialty article profiling your expertise or your products. But the specialty article is a great way to get the word out about your business, which could lead to more publicity for it and thus to more work for you.

Once the specialty article is written and proofread, it can be submitted to article databases. These are places where businesses search for relevant articles to include on their sites, blogs, and newsletters. The article is submitted once and is available for anyone to download. Your bio and contact information are included. A list of great article databases can be found in the Appendix.

<u>Advice Columns</u>

Put your knowledge of your field to work by writing an advice column. Many print publications, especially smaller ones, are constantly looking for content. Consider approaching them with a proposal to write a weekly, or even monthly, advice column. It can be in the form of readers sending in questions and you answering them, but it may be more useful for you to pick a topic that is important in your industry and share your views. An advice column is not a forum for you to get on your soapbox and spout off about your beliefs, though, rather it is a place for you to share your knowledge and advise your target market. Heck, in addition to creating buzz about your company, you may even get paid for your efforts.

Books

The pinnacle of all writing is the book. Many consider publishing a book to be the Holy Grail of publicity. Determine what you are passionate about in your business and consider spinning it into a nonfiction book as a way to market your business.

Maybe the reason people talk about getting a book published with so much awe is that they think of it as an overwhelming process or as an unachievable aspiration. Approach the writing of a book like you would any other project: take it step by step. Take it one day at a time, one proposal at a time, and one chapter at a time. Develop a rough outline for your book. Think back to what you found most interesting about your products or services when you got started and brainstorm a few ideas for chapters in your book. For example explain how you became so successful. Remember, being successful doesn't necessary mean money. It could be you have mastered the ability to balance both work and life, which is a book I'd like to read.

Query Your Book Idea

The general outline is the starting point to developing your book proposal. While there are many books on publishing nonfiction books on the market, only a select few offer this advice: send a book query letter *before* you write the whole proposal. Do not pour your time and effort into a huge proposal that may be modified by the publishing house picking up your book idea. Because you are a home-based business owner, your time is precious and it should not be wasted on putting together an extensive book proposal. Even a two-page book query letter can land a book deal. The same rules apply for book proposals as for press releases, queries, and articles; make them timely and open with a hook.

Find an Audience

If an overwhelming government statistic lets a publisher know that there is an audience for your book, you will be off to a great start. For example, according to the U.S. Census Bureau, there are 75.8 million women working from home at least eight hours a week. Those women would be interested in learning to balance work and life in their home. If your products or services can help women working from home, make them the target of your book. In other words, have an audience in mind while writing an outline, a query, or a proposal.

Solve a Problem

The next step in writing the query letter is telling the publisher what problem you are going to solve for your readers. Continuing with the example above, the book could give women specific steps to separate their work life from their home life within the general outline for the book. The outline does not need to be detailed, with each chapter and subheading profiled. Just have it describe the general idea of how you envision the book being laid out.

Once you have provided a few details of the book in your query letter, let the publisher know you have done your homework by offering existing book titles on a similar subject. Some of you are saying, "What, but then the publisher will not pick up my book because it has already been done. Right?" Wrong. You will be pointing out what those other books are missing and how your book will fill a hole in the marketplace. Providing other titles will also show you are not afraid of researching and using that research to make a point--both necessary tools when writing a book.

Be Qualified

Finally, as with the article query letter, close the book query letter by letting the publisher know you are qualified to author the book. Whether it is by stating your credentials, your past experience, or the benefits of the widget you invented, it will all add to your credibility.

While it may be difficult to find a publisher to consider your proposal, it is not impossible. Once again, certain databases, such as that of *Writer's Market,* provide you with numerous publishing houses for you to send your work to. Remember, it only takes one publisher saying "yes" for your proposal to get the green light.

Once you are published, a whole new marketing world will be open to you. Some venues will only consider having you speak if you have published a book, even if it was self-published. Speaking of self-publishing, there are whole books dedicated to the subject, so pick one up from your local library before going this route. Having a book published increases your authority, trustworthiness, and visibility. There is a reason it is seen as the pinnacle of the marketing world. Go ahead and reach for it.

Final Thoughts

Public relations may seem like a scary thing at first, but reporters, publishers, and television producers don't get together and blacklist people reaching out to the media. Using the techniques described in this chapter, you can start working on a public relations campaign. It doesn't have to be fancy or complicated. It just has to be clear, concise, and up-to-date. Remember, this is one arena where you and the big dogs compete at the same level, so get out there and start promoting your business.

10 OVERCOMING IMPLEMENTATION OBSTACLES

Remember the scenario at the beginning of the first chapter where you wander into your home office in bunny slippers, a cup of coffee in hand and people are coming to you for your products or services? Well, this is the chapter that puts it all together so that scenario becomes your reality.

The most important part of developing your marketing strategy is the implementation. Building the best marketing strategy doesn't do your business any good if the strategy sits on a shelf collecting dust. Most home-based business owners think their marketing plans needs to be complicated, long, and difficult to be put into practice. Hopefully, by reading this book, you will have realized this is the exact opposite of how a marketing strategy should be.

The marketing tools you have chosen for your business should be convenient for you to follow. If a tool doesn't work with your personality, it won't work for your business, because as a home-based business owner, you are your company. If you are the main child care provider in your family and do not have a babysitter at your beck and call or if you have agoraphobia, then choosing to attend a networking function twice a month is not a good marketing strategy for you. There are other ways to promote your business that fit within your comfort level. You need to be excited about your marketing strategy, or you won't implement it. Also by using marketing tools you enjoy, you will be more excited about your business and, in turn, create more excitement in others for it.

Use your marketing strategy to play up your personal strengths rather than your weaknesses. Some people fear public speaking more than death. If this is you, then do not have conducting a seminar as part of your marketing strategy. Rather, use tools like online networking and article writing. Or if you have a passion for sharing information but the thought of teaching a class makes you run for the bathroom, consider teaching a class online. You can still share information, but without having to stand in front of a live audience.

Using tools you absolutely cannot implement will not do any favors for your business. This does not mean you should forgo networking because your clothes are not just right or your hair is out of place, but if networking strikes fear in your heart and brings on fainting spells, then it might not be the right tool for you to grow your home-based business with. This is not a permission slip to not stretch yourself and not get out of your comfort zone. But there is a difference between being uncomfortable and being scared into inactivity.

The point is, find something in keeping with your passion for your home-based business and exploit it in as many ways as you can.

The Cost of Disorganization

Not only was the concept of clutter and disorganization useful as an example, but it really does negatively impact your success by making a marketing strategy difficult to implement. Huge amounts of time can be wasted if phone numbers can't be found to make sales calls or to follow up on leads or if contracts can't be tracked down to finalize deals or renegotiate them and especially if just finding a pen or a Post-it note on your desk seems like an insurmountable task.

Clutter takes the life out of you and your home-based business because it steals your precious time. While this is not a book on organization, here are some steps to help you reduce the clutter confusion that could stop your marketing efforts in their tracks.

The first step is to decide where you want to start. Should it be the file cabinet, the desk, the conference table, or the floor? Pick the area that is the least daunting. If you tackle the scariest place first, you might procrastinate and never start.

Now that you have decided the where, you need the how. The best advice is to tackle one area for a few minutes a day. You will be surprised how much clutter a person can get rid of in 10 to 15 minutes. And giving yourself a time limit to work in will prevent the task from feeling overwhelming. As the popular saying goes, "How do you eat an elephant? One bite at a time." During the first day of your 10-minute cleanup; find boxes for the stuff, otherwise known as clutter. It isn't going to take you the whole 10 minutes to find boxes, so label them as well. Have a box for files, receipts, and books, as well as for items that belong in other areas of your home. Just have a box for each main category of the things making up the clutter. The first day is done.

The second step is putting like things together in their designated boxes. Use as many 10-minute sessions as necessary. Once everything is sorted, make a place for the items belonging in the office by creating file folders, inserting drawer dividers, scanning important documents, and most important, using your paper shredder. Now with a place for everything to go, put it away and keep it there unless you are using it.

Once everything is said and done, you will have an amazing feeling of accomplishment, which will give you the burst of energy you will need to finish other projects involving your home-based business. Getting organized can only do one thing, and that is improving your bottom line.

If you cannot start this project on your own, have a friend hold you accountable. This may seem like an extreme measure for some, but it may give you the motivation to start the job. The hardest step is the beginning. Knowing you have to answer to someone else may keep you motivated.

Time Management

Time management seems like a simple thing to master: just do what you want with your time, right? Not so much. Either you plan your time or you will lose track of it, and it will control you. As a home-based business owner, you can waste time easily, because sometimes doing a load of laundry looks more appealing than making another sales call. It is easy to rationalize that just a few more minutes of sleep or taking a personal call won't hurt your business efforts or impact your day, but this is far from the truth.

When you set up your home-based business, you need to also set up office hours along with the number of hours you will devote to marketing. This may sound too structured for some, but you can adjust the hours to fit with your personality as well as your ideal client base. A business selling advertising whose ideal clients are restaurant or club owners is a perfect fit for a night owl. However, if you and your target market have different life schedules, you need to adjust yours to match with theirs. In other words, as a home-based business owner, you need to be disciplined about how you spend your time and determine the most effective way to use it to help you reach your target market.

Right now you may be thinking, "I have no idea how many hours I am already putting into my home-based business, and now I have to have office hours and set a specific time for marketing? Are you kidding me?" Instead of throwing the book across the room because you think you don't have time for one more thing, record the time you spend on your home-based business for one week. No cheating here. Conduct your week as usual. You might be surprised at how much time you waste doing things that aren't really important to you. Sometimes saying the word "no" is the best timesaver. There should always be time for the things that are important to you. If you don't make the time, then they are not as important to you as you thought.

Once you record a typical work week, take a look at how you are spending your time. Are there any items that are repeated during the week that can be eliminated? Do you find yourself constantly interrupted by the phone or getting distracted by e-mail? Most people these days assume they will get voicemail when they call. When you are working, use your time wisely by combining similar tasks together. For one week, try only taking and returning phone calls during certain times of the day. Do the same thing with e-mail. See if your week is more productive. Yes, emergencies come up, so a little time should be left in your day for unexpected things. The beauty of it is, if nothing comes up, you will have more time to work on your selected marketing tools.

<u>Plan</u>

A great way to get a head start on your day is by planning it the night before. It doesn't matter whether it is on paper, on your computer, or on your phone, but for 10 minutes each night or at the end of your workday, plan what needs to get done the next day. Write down everything. It doesn't all have to get done that day, but it will at least be out of your head so you won't have to keep reminding yourself to remember to do a certain task, which will free up your mind.

Once everything is written down or typed out, categorize the tasks. Make a decision as to what is most critical and what can wait. Marketing tasks should make your list every day because marketing a home-based business should be a daily process. Once you have your list sorted, accomplish the most important tasks first. Do not finish the easy items first just because you will be able to cross more items off your list. Tackle the highest priority items first and the sense of accomplishment you will feel when they are finished will propel you to complete the less important tasks.

Overcoming Procrastination

The basic definition of procrastination is putting off things that need to get done. These could be things you have to do on a regular basis or it could be a single phone call you are dreading to make. A great way to overcome procrastination is by writing down what needs to be done and why you are putting it off. Take each task and write out the worst case scenario for doing it. Then write out the best case scenario. Look at the scenarios you wrote down. Which outcome is worse? Normally the reality of doing the task falls somewhere in between the two scenarios you developed. If you are afraid of completing a task, even though by not doing it you are creating more havoc in your life as well as in your business, go back and reread the section in Chapter Two on overcoming fear.

If the scenario exercise doesn't work, try telling yourself that you only need to work for a certain amount of time and then you will get a break. It could be that you have to work for 30 minutes before you can get a 10-minute break.

Set a timer and see how much you can get done while concentrating solely on work for the specified time. It is the same method used for organizing a space: a little work, a little reward, and when you complete a lot of work, you get a big reward. Allow yourself some downtime or you will burn out.

Just as people procrastinate about organizing, they procrastinate over their list of activities because it seems overwhelming. A great exercise is to break down each task into smaller activities. On a large sheet of paper, write down the steps you need to complete a certain task on your list. Create a box for each step. Now, cut or tear the boxes into individual sheets. Pick one box each work period to complete. Finish it and then recycle it. Mentally, this makes it easier to finish a large project.

If you are a visual person, put up a picture of why you are in business to keep you motivated and on track. Is it for a certain dollar amount? Put that amount on a piece of paper and place it where you will be able to see it every day. Is it so you can spend more time with your kids? Then put a picture of your kids in a prominent place on your desk. You should have plenty of reasons for starting your business. Thinking of these will make you want to market it and make it a success.

Delegate

If you can, delegate certain tasks to make managing your time easier. Spend your time doing what you do well, and have someone else do what you find difficult, such as perhaps your accounting, billing, or receiving. Sometimes it takes people time to get up to speed on how to use certain marketing tools. In these cases, it makes sense to hire someone else to help. For example, if it will take you two days just to understand how to operate the design program for a direct mailer, hire a graphic designer; they can probably have it done in two hours. If you can't afford to delegate tasks, consider bartering your services. Use your time wisely. Once it is gone you will never get it back, no matter how hard you try to make up for it.

Benefits of Time Management

Time management is well worth the prep time it takes because of the amazing benefits you will reap. But the benefits depend on the amount of effort you are willing to put into the process. One benefit of time management is keeping you sane. When you plan your week, unexpected events don't create such critical time crunches because, if you planned well, you will have already allowed time for these unanticipated occurrences. You will also feel a greater sense of satisfaction at the end of the week because you will be able to look over your schedule and see how much you have accomplished. This in turn will lead to more productivity and energy the following week. At some point, you will find the ideal balance between activity and rest in your business, allowing you to stay excited about marketing your products or services.

Follow-Up

If you do not have a system in place for organizing potential leads, there is no point in working to fill your database with ideal clients whose information you won't be able to find. It doesn't matter if you have an electronic system or a set of three by five index cards with the contact information listed on it; the point is to have a system in place. When you get a lot of customers coming in, you will have to use an electronic database because index cards may take over your home office. Some contact management programs include ACT!, Microsoft Outlook Business Contact Manager, and Goldmine. You could even develop your own database in Excel or use QuickBooks to manage your contacts.

However you handle your database, make sure you use it. At the very least put in your client or potential client's contact information, but consider putting in short notes about how you met, what you discussed, if they purchased anything, or if they were planning on purchasing anything. You can also include personal information. This could be their birthday, the fact that their child was sick the last time you spoke, or that they were in the middle of selling their home. By asking the outcome of these events, you show that you have a personal interest in them, not only as your client, but as a person with whom you want to build a relationship.

Phone Logs

While it seems you can save an e-mail forever, voicemail is another story. Voicemail messages are deleted after a certain amount of time. Also it's useful to keep track of incoming and possibly outgoing phone calls. Once again, you can take notes in an electronic database, but sometimes you won't have time to log in to a person's file.

The answer to this is keeping a phone log. A sample phone log sheet is provided in the Appendix. Put a few sheets in a small three-ring binder. Keep the binder in a convenient place so you can take notes while you talk or jot down when you call a potential client. A really nice thing about phone logs is that if you have a dispute with a client, either inside or outside legal proceedings, you have a written log backing up your end of the deal.

Marketing Calendar

Marketing success is a combination of consistent and persistent preparation. No matter which marketing tools you choose to work with, make sure to use them consistently. To be persistent in tracking your marketing efforts, establish a marketing calendar. You probably already have a calendar for your appointments. If you do not, consider picking up a book on organizing your business. This chapter will touch on some organization tips that can turn you into a marketing machine. Using your marketing tools should be just another item on your calendar.

A marketing calendar should list tasks to be accomplished over the next six months to a year, and the order in which they need to be completed. Have a completion date for each task. If the marketing tools you choose need to be completed in several steps, break the overall goal down into simple tasks.

For example, if you don't have a website yet, deciding on a domain name that corresponds with your business, reserving the name, writing content, and finding or creating graphics are just a few of the things needed before the website can be up and running for the entire world to see. These tasks can be placed individually on your calendar to make the goal of having a website manageable.

Any tasks that need attending to before your marketing tools can be implemented should be part of your marketing calendar.

As discussed before, especially when you are starting out, do something every day. Even if it is only for 15 minutes a day, your business will be ahead of most home-based businesses if you do so. Do not fool yourself into thinking you can set aside one day a week to market your business. Things pop up and it will be too easy to blow off marketing until the next week. If you make an appointment every day to call a few people, work on your press release, submit an article or your sales letters, then you are more likely to accomplish your goals.

Post your marketing calendar where you can see it every day. Don't put it on a bookshelf or file it away. If there is a lull in your day you can immediately start working on your marketing strategy because it will be easy for you to pick up where you left off once your next steps are already laid out.

<u>Marketing Partners</u>

If you just cannot keep yourself motivated to do marketing on a daily basis, get a marketing partner. A marketing partner, or a marketing coach, is a person or a group of people holding you responsible for starting, working on, or finishing your marketing tasks.

Opportunities to find a marketing partner abound. Whether it is a professional marketing coach, one of your strategic business partners, a business coach, a life coach, a close friend, or even your significant other, ask them to hold you accountable for reaching your goals. Just make sure that they are the type of person who will give you a cheerleader speech or a quick, swift kick in your derrière if you are not doing what needs to be done.

Developing a strategy and implementing that strategy on a consistent basis will bring your business success. As with most important things in life, marketing your home-based business is a marathon, not a sprint. Reaching your marketing goals will not happen overnight. If it were easy, everyone would be a success. If you are in business for the long-term, your marketing strategy needs to grow and work with you.

Building a Better Client Relationship

Just for review, the first four of the five "P's" in marketing are product, price, place, and promotion. Rarely do marketing books talk about building your business and working with the most important "P" in the five "P's" of marketing. That elusive "P" stands for people. The relationship between yourself and your clients is the lifeblood of your home-based business. Keeping in touch with your clients is just the starting point of building better relationships with them. Think of the television show *The Million Dollar Man*, where each piece creates a better, stronger, faster man. Keeping the following steps in mind will help you build better, stronger, and faster relationships with your existing as well as potential clients.

Having a Clear Vision

Socrates once said, "Know thyself." This leads back to Chapter Two where it was explained that having a clear vision of your company is essential. As a home-based business owner, you can easily fall into the trap of trying to be all things to all people. By knowing what you will or will not do, you will create a better relationship with your client.

For example, if you are computer programmer who can do website design, but who does not enjoy the process, offering to design for a client as well would take more out of you than it is worth. If you have not established a strategic partnership with a graphic designer who creates layouts quickly, as well as easily, then you may disappoint your client by not delivering their website in a professional, timely manner. Damage control will then be needed in your client relationship. It is simpler to be upfront and honest with your clients about your abilities instead of risking disappointing them. A great rule in working with clients is to under promise and over deliver. It is perfectly acceptable to tell clients that while you do not specialize in a specific area, your strategic business partner is an expert in that field. Then set up a meeting with all parties and serve as the project manager. It is a win, win for everyone and you will be creating a trusting relationship with your client because you were honest and upfront about your strengths and abilities.

Don't Be Desperate

The next step in building a better client relationship is to not appear desperate. This relates to knowing what you will or will not do in your business. Having confidence in your skills, abilities, and what your business offers will make your products or services even more attractive to potential customers.

Don't constantly call on your client. It is great to check in, but do not call them every day to find out whether they have made a decision about your products or services. They may start thinking that they are your only possible client and get a little nervous that your products or services are not as great as they thought.

Keeping in contact with a client means consistently dripping information on them. Ask your potential and current clients how much contact makes them feel comfortable. Some customers want to hear from you on a weekly basis for updates and information, while others view monthly phone calls, newsletters, or handwritten notes as intrusive. Consider your clients' needs and customize your methods of interaction to fit their desires. Rarely do large corporations offer this type of customer service, and as a home-based business owner, you have the advantage of being able to treat your potential and current clients as individuals as opposed to numbers in a file.

Establish an Equal Relationship

You and your client are equals because they need or want what you have, and you need or want what they have to offer in exchange. Many home-based business owners approach their potential customers with their hats in hand and almost grovel to make the sale. Doing this is ridiculous. Be confident, but not arrogant, and your clients will respect you all the more. When you are confident in offering your products or services, there will automatically be a sense of confidence around your marketing. Do not be a doormat.

Establishing an equal relationship from the beginning is also important when you are negotiating the prices for your products or services. Unless your prices are set by a franchise or a resale company, you will be negotiating every purchase or contract. This is when it is most critical to have a client respect you and your offerings.

For example, let's say you find a client by doing some cold calling. You are excited about meeting the client, only to find out at the meeting they want to lowball the price you discussed on the phone, indicating that they don't value a relationship with you and are just looking for a cheap way to obtain your products or services. Make the decision to stick to your price, or have the guts to walk away. If the potential customer sees you cave on the price you agreed on over the phone, they will continually come back and ask you to reduce your price because they won't respect the relationship. Move on to a client who is looking for a long-term and evenly balanced partnership.

Be Honest

Above all, when you are building a better client relationship, be honest. Tell the client what they need to hear. Your client bought your products or services because they thought it would make their current state better. If it will not, tell them the truth.

For example, if you work in advertising sales and you know that a potential advertiser is in the wrong market for your publication, tell them. The word of mouth about your honesty will mean more than any marketing dollars you could spend.

Keep Current Clients Happy

Finally, keep your existing clients happy. It is much harder and takes more energy as well as money to get new clients than to keep the ones you already have. Keep building on existing relationships. Constantly bring value to your client relationships. How do you do that?

For example, a regional land use nonprofit organization needed creative ways to get their trail cleaned up without spending critical donation dollars. An article appeared in a national magazine about using cleanup projects as team building exercises for corporate executives. The article fit perfectly in the parameters of the client's needs and they appreciated the thoughtfulness of their consultant passing the article along with a short handwritten note on how it could benefit their organization.

Customer Service

One of the best ways to keep your marketing efforts rolling is through excellent customer service. Having great customer service gives your home-based business two benefits: the first is loyal customers; the second is great referral resources. Chapter Seven covered how to ask for a referral, but this section will cover how to supply great customer service that is not just done through lip service or empty marketing slogans.

There are many benefits to being in business for yourself, such as being able to choose which clients you want to work with. But don't withdraw from a customer because they have a complaint about your business. Think of the complaint as constructive criticism, take it with a dash of reality, and use it to your advantage.

<u>Keep It Easy</u>

Make it easy for customers to complain. Offer comment cards online or telephone surveys as outlets for your customers to voice their opinions. If your customer is too scared or embarrassed to share a complaint with you personally, make it easy for them to offer suggestions anonymously through your webpage or through a direct mailing of a customer satisfaction survey. Their honest feedback will make you a lean, mean marketing machine because you will know the hot buttons of your target market. The more thorough you encourage the feedback to be, the better you can tailor your marketing message to your ideal customer and the better products or services you will provide.

<u>Handling a Complaint</u>

How you handle a complaint will speak volumes to your client and may lead to repeat business as well as word-of-mouth advertising. Remember the saying, "The customer is always right"? While they may not be right all the time, treat them as if they are. You cannot win an argument with a customer because all they will hear is you not meeting their needs and the company they paid their hard-earned cash to not taking steps to resolve their problem.

To the best of your ability, resolve their complaint on the first contact rather than dragging the process out. The more a problem is dragged out, the more resources are taken up working with the client, and the more irritated the client will get. They are now telling their family, friends, letter carrier, checkout person, and anyone else who will listen what a horrible company they had to work with. Various customer satisfaction surveys have found that dissatisfied customers tell between seven and ten people about their problems. This is not the kind of word-of-mouth advertising you want spreading about your business. Fix the problem fast and you may have a customer singing your praises rather than cursing the day they heard of your company.

Thinking "Relatively"

When working through a problem with a customer, think of them as a relative. Not the relative you avoid every holiday or family get-together, but the family member or friend you can't wait to spend time with and would do anything to protect. Treat your complaining client as you would treat any valuable person in your life. Listen to the problem--the entire problem--without interruption. This will make the person feel heard and in turn you will have all the information you will need to respond accordingly.

Even if their complaint or bad attitude is unfounded, there is something going on that is making them unhappy with the products or services they received. Get to the root of the problem by asking them questions about their experience and responding to their rude behavior with kindness as well as respect. It may turn out they are not really unhappy with your company, but that their spouse just left them and you are taking the brunt of their anger. You may not be able to fix the underlying issue, but you can respond to a complaining customer with an attitude of opportunity rather than one of indifference or defensiveness.

Marketing to existing customers that are already happy with your customer service and business practices is a simple, cost-effective way to increase your business because these people have already bought from you and are already building a relationship with you. Make providing great customer service a way of doing business rather than a marketing slogan. By having loyal customers as well as walking advertisers for your home-based business, your marketing will be made easier.

Final Thoughts

Creating your marketing strategy and overcoming obstacles to implementing it are only the first steps in building a successful home-based business. The most important step is taking the time on a consistent and persistent basis to implement your marketing strategy. This is the only way to make your dreams of owning a successful and profitable home-based business a reality.

11 MARKETING REVIEWS AND RESULTS

Now that you know how to overcome obstacles while implementing your marketing strategy, you need to know how to review your results once you have put that strategy into effect. Back in Chapter Two you laid out your goals and objectives for your business. This is the step where those goals and objectives meet your marketing strategy. The clearer your goals and objectives, the easier it will be to measure the results of your marketing efforts.

Measuring Profitability

All the marketing tools in the world and the best implementation strategy won't do your home-based business any good unless you can bring checks to the bank. Measuring the profitability of your home-based business is essential in developing a marketing strategy and is vital to your business being a success story, rather than another failed business statistic.

Evaluating Marketing Tools

Review your marketing efforts approximately once a month, but do not give up on a marketing tool if it doesn't work directly out of the gate. Though you may have placed advertisements in front of your target market, it may take up to six exposures for people to begin calling you. Give each marketing tool about six attempts before giving up on it.

When a marketing tool isn't working for your home-based business, ask yourself if you are using the tool in the best possible way. Using the advertisement example again, if the ad is placed in a periodical that is marginally relevant to your target market, it might not be as effective as if a little more research is put into the demographic of the periodical, revealing that only 30 percent of the readership is in your target market. The advertisement may communicate to your target audience, but it won't reach them because it is placed in the wrong area.

Part of evaluating your marketing plan is setting up your expectations for the particular marketing tool you have chosen to implement. That is, you should create goals and objectives not only for your business, but for your marketing tools as well. Then take those marketing tools and break down the costs of each to assess your achievements.

Evaluating Your ROI

The cost verses benefit of marketing is rather simple to track. Based on how much you spend on a given marketing tool, you can determine what your return is, otherwise known as the ROI, or the return on investment.

Don't forget the cost of your time. As a home-based business owner, it is easy to write off a marketing tool as free if it didn't cost any money. The problem with this is that it dismisses all the time that was put into it. Time is the one commodity you can never get back or renew; make sure to use it wisely and with getting the best return in mind.

For example, let's say you spent $400 sending out post cards to people who met your requirements for an ideal client. Because of the post cards, you received $600 in sales. So your overall ROI is $200.

Simple, right? So why do many home-based business owners not calculate this? Because they don't believe they have the time or the resources to track their marketing. But nothing could be further from the truth. Because you wear the hat of the marketing manager of your home-based business, you need to justify your costs and efforts. If you were working for someone else and could not directly show any profit from your marketing efforts, you wouldn't last long in the company. Do not operate the marketing of your home-based business any differently than you would if you were working for someone else. Tracking your ROI is just a matter of record keeping.

Use a spreadsheet to find your ROI for each marketing tool you use. Determine the amount of time you spend on a marketing tool, otherwise known as a soft cost, and don't underestimate. Home-based business owners have a tendency to reduce their time because they multitask while they are working on their marketing. Even if you only work 15 minutes a day on marketing and with interruptions, keep track of exactly how much marketing you are doing. Then keep track of your hard costs, or any money spent on materials, postage, mileage, or meetings. Finally, determine which products or services were sold based on which marketing tools. The best way to find this out is by asking your customers how they heard about your business. Even if people don't buy your products or services, ask them how they heard about you when they contact you. It is then up to you as CEO of your home-based business to determine if the ROI is worth the effort the next time around. In Chapter Twelve there is a Marketing Costs Tracker Sheet.

Price Adjustment

Reviewing your marketing tools also includes reviewing the price of your products or services. How much you need to earn from each customer depends on which marketing tools you have chosen for your marketing strategy. For example, if you are advertising in glossy, high-profile magazines, you must offer products or services at prices that cover not only your operating costs, but your marketing costs as well. Finding out how much your home-based business is spending to obtain each client is critical to staying in the black and having success for years to come.

Determining how much you are spending on each customer is relatively easy; it just requires a little sleuthing: Ask your customers why they decided to do business with you. This is something that could be included in your customer satisfaction survey, discussed in Chapter Eight.

If you do business with friends and relatives, then it is pretty easy to determine that you are the deciding factor in their purchasing decisions.

However, if you are doing business with people you meet at networking events, through word-of-mouth referrals, because of articles, or through advertising, then you can calculate how much you invested in each of those marketing tools and how much you earned from each contact with your client.

For example, let's say you met a potential client at a networking event. You really hit it off and decided to meet for coffee the following week. Based on the information from the networking event, you develop a sales presentation for the coffee meeting. After meeting for coffee, the potential client is interested but has to wait a few months for their company budget to be finalized. You then ask to include them on your monthly electronic newsletter and offer to call once a month to follow up about the possible sale. Your potential client agrees. At the end of six months, the company signs the deal.

So how much was spent to get this client? It breaks down like this:

$20 for the networking event

$120 for the time and materials to put together a sales presentation

$8 for coffee

$100 for your time to meet with the potential client

$30 for each time you sent an electronic newsletter. In this scenario, it was six times. (The exact cost of how much of what you spend on an electronic newsletter is put forth in obtaining one client is difficult to determine since the newsletter goes out to existing clients as well as to potential clients. To get a more accurate cost, divide the number of potential clients by the total subscribers to your newsletter.)

$20 for your time each month you called. Once again, in this scenario, it was six times.

In total, it cost $548 to obtain your client. Did they buy enough to cover your costs or do you need to reevaluate the price of your products or services?

Be aware that pricing depends on many factors, not just on the costs of obtaining clients. However, to know how much is going out, you need to keep this factor in mind.

<u>Fixing a Marketing Tool</u>

While you may not see the results you want from the marketing tools you choose for your home-based business, don't be too quick to change everything at once. Look at your Marketing Costs Tracker Sheet to find out which marketing tools you have invested the most in and seen the least return for. Remember, this also includes time you put in.

Switch out the underperforming marketing tool with another marketing tool, but only if you have given it enough time and implemented it as best as you could. Make changes slowly. Modify marketing tools one at a time so you can evaluate what really isn't working and what just needs tweaking.

Payment

Before you launch into expanding your business through your marketing efforts, think about how you want your customers to pay.

Do you prefer they pay by check, by credit card, or through an online system like PayPal? This will make a difference in your bottom line. If you only want people to pay by check, you may leave a customer no other option than to go to your competition because that company accepts credit cards.

However, when you accept credit cards the credit card companies take a chunk of your profits for the privilege of using their service. Will you charge your customers extra for using credit cards? (Businesses normally add around three percent to the cost of services or goods.) Or will you consider it a cost of doing business?

Determine what is best for your customers. If your home-based business sells high-priced products or services, many companies or individuals won't be able to cover that cost without credit cards. Once again, ask your clients what they think. You may find out that offering different payment methods is all that stands between you and more sales without you having to spend additional dollars on marketing.

Learn from Mistakes

The best lessons home-based business owners learn may come from the mistakes they make implementing marketing tools. Turn your mistakes into lessons that will help you create a more profitable company in the future.

Sometimes marketing tools don't work because of simple, silly mistakes, such as putting the wrong contact information in marketing communications. For example, a public relations firm got one number wrong in the 1-800 number in their advertisement. That one wrong number sent their potential customers to an adult entertainment establishment. So what does a good public relations company do? The company spun it into a funny story for *Entrepreneur* and received great free national publicity. They learned from their mistake and worked it to their benefit.

Again, when a marketing tool does not work as you expect it to, do not immediately write it off. Look at how the marketing tool was used. Do its colors need to be modified slightly? Does it need better copy? Should it be placed somewhere else? Was the right target market profiled? Ask some of your reliable existing customers what they like or don't like about the marketing tool you are currently using. Hopefully they will provide you with honest answers so you can rework your strategy based on their feedback.

Learn from Success

When your marketing tools are working, celebrate, and then find out why. What made your potential clients pick up the phone, drop an e-mail, or visit your website? Once again, ask them. People don't mind if you ask them how they heard of you. While you could wait until someone fills out a customer satisfaction survey, it is best to just find out the information immediately when customers make initial contact. If you met a customer over time, then break down which tools you used and how much they cost, like in the price adjustment example, to determine which marketing tools or combination of marketing tools led to your success.

Continue Learning

Never stop learning. Whether you read up on different marketing tools, research your target market, or tweak your website, continue to build on the knowledge you acquire. Not only has the technology revolution enabled home-based business owners to do what they do so well from home, but with the ease of obtaining information, there is no excuse for not keeping tabs on new trends in your industry.

The path toward reaching your goal of increasing your business through better marketing doesn't end with reading this book. To obtain the success you desire, try to read or research something about your products or services on a weekly or even daily basis. This may mean less time in front of the television or less time surfing the Internet for fun, but the payoff is having a successful home-based business you can pass on to your family or sell to the highest bidder.

Get Mentored

When your marketing is not working the way you

envisioned, consider finding a mentor willing to work with you and answer any questions you may have on how to build your business. This is different than finding a mentor amongst your competition as discussed in Chapter Five. This person doesn't have to work in your industry or be in your target market, but they do have to be someone whom you admire for their business success. This person should be someone who is willing to help you through the rough times you will face while building your home-based business, someone you can ask questions without the fear of being belittled and be open as well as honest with while receiving the same treatment in return.

SCORE

The SCORE program (www.score.org) is based on this premise, and it is free. They will offer you confidential one-on-one business counseling sessions for as long as you need. Depending on your needs, you fill out a form online and wait to be paired with a counselor who is either a retired businessperson or someone currently running their own company. With this person, you can discuss just about every aspect of starting and running your home-based business. SCORE even offers business workshops on numerous subjects about developing a business.

Chambers of Commerce

Finding a person or a group of people like this is not as difficult as you might think. Some chambers of commerce offer programs where, within a group counseling session, you can air whatever business problems you may be having in a safe environment. The same group meets on a regular basis and is led by someone who has been there, done that, so to speak, and can offer advice on overcoming obstacles to your success.

Finding Your Own Mentor

You can also find a mentor on your own. When approaching a potential mentor, realize they are very busy and might only have limited time to offer, so approach them as you would a potential client. Let them know why you want to work with them. Answer why they should take time out of their busy schedule to mentor you. Be willing to work with them and implement any advice they give you. As a final selling point, remind them how tough it was when they started out, and tell them you would love to have the benefit of their experience and knowledge to make your business a success. Even if they can only meet with you once, take it. If they are so busy, meeting is out of the question, offer to correspond over the phone or through e-mail. The more you can accommodate them, the more willing a person will be to help you.

Once you find a mentor, here are some possible questions to ask:

What are the most valuable lessons you have learned about being successful?

What was most helpful to you when you were learning the ropes?

What are the biggest mistakes to avoid and the greatest obstacles to overcome?

How did you find clients?

What marketing tools worked best for you?

Do you ever budge on a price quote?

Should I be charging the market minimum?

If you could give only one piece of advice to someone who wanted to do what you do, what would it be?

Having a mentor is an invaluable asset to your company. Not only can they encourage you when you are going through a difficult time, but they can offer you advice on how to get beyond the trials and move on to victory.

<u>Marketing Burnout</u>

As a home-based business owner, you can never get away from your office, which could lead to burnout. When you are frustrated or discouraged with your business, which will happen from time to time, you cannot market it effectively. By taking care of yourself, you can avoid burnout.

First, give yourself a break. Most successful home-based business owners are driven, and they may drive themselves into the ground. Allow yourself one day a week where you won't work on anything business related. Spend time away from your home office by going out with family or friends or by doing an activity you enjoy.

Second, exercise on a regular basis. Not only will this allow you to get into better shape, but it will provide you a mental break. This doesn't mean you have to attend an intense class that makes it so you can barely move the next day. Instead, you could take a walk around your block, stroll through the shopping mall, or visit a gym for a light workout. It is most important for you to find an activity you enjoy enough that you will do it regularly.

Third, give yourself permission to make mistakes. No one is perfect and you can burn out by trying to achieve marketing perfection. Marketing collateral can only be proofread so many times; it eventually needs to be sent out or it won't do your business any good. So what if you make a mistake at a presentation? Laugh it off or make amends the best you can and move on with your business. Dwelling on past missteps won't do you any good. Forgive yourself and strive to do better in the future.

The Marketing Egg Basket

When picking out which marketing tools to use, do not put all your eggs in one basket. Using many small marketing tools will be much more effective for your business than just using one big tool. Think about companies like Coca-Cola. They have commercials, sponsor events, place products in movies and in television, and have corporate partnerships with restaurants around the world, just to name a few of the tools in their marketing arsenals. You probably don't have the marketing budget of the Coca-Cola Corporation, but you can do similar things on a smaller scale. Great marketing is about having a multipronged approach, implementing it on a consistent as well as a persistent basis, and then evaluating the results.

Final Thoughts

Having a marketing strategy you can execute on a

consistent and persistent basis, which you are excited about implementing, will be the difference between success and failure. Remember, whether they are for your benefit or demise, the choices you make today impact your tomorrow. Make the choice to work on your marketing strategy every day, and you will be a home-based business success story.

12 MARKETING TOOL SAMPLES

Letter of Introduction

October 28, 2013

Jane Doe

123 Main Street

Anywhere, CO 80124

Dear Jane:

It was a pleasure meeting you at XYZ event. Since you showed an interest in our company, I wanted to follow up with you and provide a brief background of our company.

Lavish Touch Massage Therapy is a full service massage therapy business offering the advantage the appointments in your home or office. Since we travel to you we allow even the busiest person a chance to unwind.

With experience in outstanding customer service, I believe

our business will serve your needs or the needs of your friends and family. At Lavish Touch Massage Therapy, we welcome the opportunity to make an ongoing or occasional contribution to your relaxation efforts and feel confident in our ability to reduce the stress in your life.

Please feel free to contact me at any time to begin a relaxation retreat.

Sincerely,

Nancy Jones

Certified Massage Therapist

Letter to the Editor

October 28, 2013

Jane Doe

123 Main Street

Anywhere, CO 80124

Dear Jane:

In the October 2005 edition of *Relaxation Today*, the article "Building Your Therapeutic Massage Business – One Rub at a Time," offered tips on marketing and advertising for therapeutic massage businesses from industry experts. While the marketing ideas proposed in the article are solid business practices, the complied comments did not include the value of building relationships as part of expanding your business. For example at Lavish Touch Massage Therapy, we have a referral program that gives 15 minutes of treatment for each new customer our existing client brings to the business.

It is the personal touches that allow a business to stand out in an over-marketed world.

Please feel free to contact me if *Relaxation Today* is ever in need of quotes or sources for massage therapy articles. You may reach me by e-mail at <u>Nancy@LavishTouch.com</u> or by phone at (303) 555-7735.

Sincerely,

Nancy Jones

Certified Massage Therapist

Media Release for Opening of Business

FOR IMMEDIATE RELEASE

Date: May 23, 2013

Contact: Nancy Jones

Telephone: (303) 555-7735

Email: <u>Nancy@LavishTouch.com</u>

Lavish Touch Opens for Business

Anywhere, CO, May 23, 2013 – Lavish Touch is pleased to announce the opening of their business. Lavish Touch

Massage Therapy offers the relaxing advantage of a full therapeutic massage experience but with the convenience of appointments in the client's home.

Those interested in obtaining more information on the services offered by Lavish Touch Massage Therapy should call (303) 555-7735.

Lavish Touch Massage Therapy

P.O. Box 1234

Anywhere, CO 80163

www.lavishtouch.com

Media Release for Award, Special Announcement

FOR IMMEDIATE RELEASE

Date: October 28, 2013

Contact: Nancy Jones

Telephone: (303) 555-7735

Email: Nancy@LavishTouch.com

Lavish Touch Massage Therapy Unveils Results of $15,000 Mega-Marketing Makeover Contest

Anywhere, CO, December 18, 2013 – Lavish Touch Massage Therapy is pleased to announce the re-branding of their business in conjunction with being selected as the grand prize winner for the Mega-Marketing Makeover Contest. The grand unveiling celebration took place on December 17, 2013 at the Chamber of Commerce. To see their revised image, visit the website at www.lavishtouch.com.

Lavish Touch Massage Therapy offers the relaxing advantage of a full therapeutic massage experience but with the convenience of appointments in the client's home.

Those interested in obtaining more information on the services offered by Lavish Touch Massage Therapy should call (303) 555-7735.

Lavish Touch Massage Therapy

P.O. Box 1234

Anywhere, CO 80163

www.lavishtouch.com

<u>Referral Program Letter</u>

October 28, 2013

Jane Doe

123 Main Street

Anywhere, CO 80124

Dear Jane:

Thank you for taking the time to enjoy one of Lavish Touch Massage Therapy's services. It was our pleasure to help you relax. Since you spoke so highly of our services, we would like to inform you of our referral program.

Lavish Touch Massage Therapy's referral program provides a benefit to you as well as to us. Our referral program provides an experience your friends, family and co-workers won't soon forget and it allows you the opportunity to earn more relaxation time. For each person that you refer to Lavish Touch Massage Therapy, you will receive 15 minutes towards any future therapeutic massage.

If you know any of your friends, family or co-workers that need a little relaxation time, please tell them about Lavish Touch Massage Therapy and our relaxation options.

Contact me today to begin participating in our referral program.

Sincerely,

Nancy Jones

Certified Massage Therapist

<u>Referral Request Letter</u>

October 28, 2013

Jane Doe

123 Main Street

Anywhere, CO 80124

Dear Jane:

I am very excited to share with you my home based business venture. Lavish Touch Massage Therapy is a full service massage therapy business offering the advantage of appointments in your home or office. Since we travel to you we allow even the busiest person a chance to unwind.

With experience in outstanding customer service, I believe our business will serve your needs or the needs of your friends and family. At Lavish Touch Massage Therapy, we welcome the opportunity to make an ongoing or occasional contribution to your relaxation efforts and feel confident in our ability to reduce the stress in your life.

Please feel free to contact me at any time to begin a relaxation retreat.

Sincerely,

Nancy Jones

Certified Massage Therapist

Request for Testimonial Letter

October 28, 2013

Jane Doe

123 Main Street

Anywhere, CO 80124

Dear Jane:

We are happy you enjoyed your therapeutic massage with Lavish Touch Massage Therapy. Since you mentioned how much you adored your time with us, we are requesting a written testimonial about your experience. To make the testimonial letter worth your time, we are offering you a complimentary 30 minute chair massage therapy session.

Feel free to e-mail it or mail it to:

Nancy@LavishTouch.com

or

Lavish Touch Massage Therapy

Attn: Nancy Jones

P.O. Box 1234

Anywhere, CO 80163

Thank you in advance for your time.

Sincerely,

Nancy Jones

Certified Massage Therapist

Story Pitch

October 28, 2013

Fox News

Attn: Jane Doe

123 Main Street

Denver, CO 80202

Dear Ms. Jones,

Nancy Jones is not the type of person to take the words, "It can't be done," to heart. Instead, she asks, "Why not?" and then proceeds to show how it can be done. When she couldn't find a massage therapist that fit her active lifestyle, she launched Lavish Touch, a traveling massage therapy business.

Even though she had no experience in the massage therapy industry, she didn't let that stop her. Nancy began by calling other massage therapists in the Denver area and asked them how they did business. Surprisingly, they were candid about the industry and provided her with an abundance of information to help get her company started from where to obtain education and where to find clients.

As a professor at the University of Colorado in Boulder and busy mom, Nancy is not the typical massage therapist. She doesn't even consider herself a massage therapist, she thinks of herself as giving a healing touch. In her mind, massage therapy is not just about relaxing but providing a doorway to a healthier lifestyle. According to Nancy, "It's not just a person on my massage table; it's about the giving a better life to each woman I help feel better."

If you are interested in obtaining more information on Nancy Jones and Lavish Touch please call 303-555-7735, e-mail Nancy@LavishTouch.com or surf their website at www.LavishTouch.com. Thank you for your time and consideration of Lavish Touch.

Sincerely,

Kris Valdez

Independent PR Consultant

P.O. Box 1413

Gypsum, CO 81637

Phone: 303-868-3789

E-mail: Kris.Valdez10@gmail.com

Source Letter

April 20, 2013

Relaxation Today

Attn: Jane Doe, Managing Editor

123 ABC St., Ste. 300

Denver, CO 80202

Dear Ms. Doe:

If you or your writers need a quote or an article from a certified massage therapist, specifically concerning ways for women to relax, please contact me. I understand the deadlines writers are under to get a story out on time with reliable sources and I can help alleviate some of that deadline stress by being a local reference for you or your writers to use. For your future reference, let me provide you with a brief background of my business.

Lavish Touch Massage Therapy is a full service massage therapy business offering the advantage the appointments in your home or office. Since I travel to my clients I allow even the busiest person a chance to unwind and live a healthier lifestyle.

Please contact us at any time and feel free to look at our website www.lavishtouch.com. Thank you for your consideration. You may reach me by e-mail at nancy@lavishtouch.com or by phone at 303-555-7735.

Sincerely,

Nancy Jones

Certified Massage Therapist

Article Query Sample

Attn: Laura Kalehoff

Self

Condé Nast
4 Times Square
New York, NY 10036

RE: Article Query with Proposed Title: Are You
Financially Ready To Commit?

April 13, 2013

Dear Ms. Kalehoff:

When we think of relationships, for women especially, the
idea that love conquers all is the fairytale we believe. Very
few women look at their financial situation before taking
the plunge into a committed relationship. Arguing about
who is taking out the garbage tonight is a minor problem
compared to who is planning on paying the rent this
month or deciding if bank accounts will be combined.
Women must examine their own financial house before
they move into their partner's house.

According to The National Marriage Project at New Jersey's Rutgers University, the U.S. marriage rate is on a steady decline: a 50% drop since 1970 from 76.5 per 1,000 unmarried women to 39.9 in 2005. This means that more and more couples are choosing to live together, rather than get married, but the financial implications are still significant. The study also indicates that women are more likely to remain divorced longer than men because men remarry sooner. Thus, it is more important for women to have information about the impact their relationship could have on their financial future.

Most couples fight over money. Howard Dettloff, a financial consultant with over 30 years of experience dispensing advice about money, says many couples have problems communicating about money. They don't disclose their financial needs, wants, and desires before they commit. Mr. Dettloff offers a few pieces of advice to women before entering a long term relationship. Some of the ideas include:

Talk about your budget expectations

Discuss different spending and saving patterns

Don't play the blame game when or if things get tough financially

Talk about what things are financially important to them

Discuss how much debt you and your partner will be taking into the relationship.

This article would be of interest to your readership because 96 percent are women and 51 percent are not married. Whether they are in their first committed relationship or moving into a secondary relationship after a divorce, women should know how to protect themselves and the assets they bring to a relationship.

I currently write a bi-monthly column, entitled "Mom Share" for *Lone Tree Magazine*. The website is www.LoneTreeMagazine.com I have also written for national trade magazines, *Museum Store Association* and *Planning*. Regionally, I have been published in the *Denver Business Journal* and repeatedly in *Women's Edition*. If you would like to see my published clips as well as a letter of recommendation from the editor at *Women's Edition*, I would be happy to forward those to you. Thank you for your consideration. You may reach me by e-mail at Kris.Valdez10@gmail.com or by phone at 303-868-3789.

Sincerely,

Kris Valdez

P.O. Box 1413

Gypsum, CO 81637

303-868-3789

Class/Speaking/Seminar Evaluation Sheet

Are you relaxed? How to stay sane and healthy this holiday season

Speaker: Nancy Jones – Certified Massage Therapist with Lavish Touch

November 15, 2013

Please circle the number which best expresses your reaction to each of the items below, with 5 rated the highest

The ideas/activities were interesting: 5 4 3 2 1

The content was interesting: 5 4 3 2 1

The instructor was organized & prepared: 5 4 3 2 1

Materials & handouts were current: 5 4 3 2 1

Facilities were appropriate: 5 4 3 2 1

Topics on the course outline were taught: 5 4 3 2 1

The information I received should prove meaningful:

5 4 3 2 1

Did this class/seminar meet your expectations?
Yes_____ No_____

What are your biggest frustrations about using a massage therapist?

_____

_____

_____
_____
_____
_____
_____
_____

Would you like this class to be a monthly
offering?_____

If yes, what topics would you like to see
covered?_____

_____

Lavish Touch is launching a free electronic monthly
marketing tip sheet. Would you be interested in
subscribing? Yes_____ No_____

E-Mail Address:_____

Other comments?

_____
_____
_____
_____

Your Name:_____

Phone number:_____

Email Address (Please Print)_____

Thank you for your time!

Customer Satisfaction Survey for a Comment Card

Overall, how would you rate Lavish Touch?

Excellent

Good

Average

Poor

Terrible

Not Sure

How satisfied are you with your (product or service) from Lavish Touch?

Extremely Satisfied

Very Satisfied

Neutral

Very Dissatisfied

Extremely dissatisfied

Would you recommend Lavish Touch to a friend or another business?

Yes

No

Not Sure

If no, why not?

How likely are you to use Lavish Touch again?

Definitely would use

Probably would use

Might or might not use

Probably would not use

Definitely would not use

If you would not use Lavish Touch again, why not?

Do you have any other comments for Lavish Touch?

Sample Marketing Telephone Survey

How did you hear about Lavish Touch?

What specifically made you decide to contact Lavish Touch?

What was the best part about your massage with Lavish Touch?

What was the most difficult part about working with Lavish Touch?

Would you get a massage from Lavish Touch again? Why or why not?

On a scale of one to five, with one being least important

and five being the most important, please indicate how important each of the following aspects are in choosing massage therapist:

Service…..1 2 3 4 5

Existing relationship…..1 2 3 4 5

Referral…..1 2 3 4 5

Location…..1 2 3 4 5

Price…..1 2 3 4 5

Special offers…..1 2 3 4 5

Marketing and Customer Service Script for an Independent Survey

(Have a friend call on behalf of your business if you don't want to hire someone)

Ask for the participant by name

(Participant's name), please

Say hello using the participant's name

Hi, (participant's name).

Identify my company

My name is Kris Valdez. I'm with Novel Ideas. Did I catch you at a good time?

Say why I am calling

I am a marketing consultant working with Lavish Touch and I just wanted a few minutes of your time and briefly ask you some questions about Lavish Touch. Will that work or should we schedule another time to talk? All of your responses will be kept confidential and only the results, not names, will be given to Lavish Touch.

Begin marketing questions

See Sample Marketing Telephone Survey

Thank participant for their time

(Participant's name), I know you are incredibly busy and I want to thank you for taking the time to speak with me today. If I have any more questions or need clarification on your answers, would it be alright to contact you at a later date? (Wait for answer) Thank you again for your time.

Marketing Telephone Survey Results Sample

How did you hear about Lavish Touch?

Knew Nancy Jones (15 responses)

From ad in *Relaxation Today (10 responses)*

Knew Nancy Jones from the Chamber of Commerce events (5 responses)

Jim Doe referred me (2)

What specifically made you decide to work with Lavish Touch?

Because of Nancy's personality and skills (15 responses)

Had an existing relationship with Nancy (10 responses)

Knew Nancy (5 responses)

Needed a massage for a relaxation party in my home (2 responses)

What was the best part about working with Lavish Touch?

Feeling better, more relaxed, able to move again (10 responses)

Saving time by not driving to massage (10 responses)

Quality of service (5 responses)

Felt comfortable working with Nancy (5 responses)

What was the most difficult part about working with Lavish Touch?

Nothing (30 responses)

Too expensive (2 responses)

Would you work with Lavish Touch again? Why or why not?

Yes (28 responses)

Because of Nancy (12 responses)

Because of the way I feel afterwards (12 responses)

Because of convenience (2 responses)

Because of excellent service (2 responses)

No

Too expensive for service (1 response)

Didn't like having someone in my home (1 response)

Below is a summary of responses for question six.

	1	2	3	4	5
Service				3	27
Existing Relationships			10	10	10
Referral			9	11	10
Location	30				
Price	1	1	9	9	10
Special Offers	5	5	10	5	5

So what does this short survey tell you about your business? First, people are using your business because they know the owner and feel comfortable with her. In response to this information, Nancy Jones should continue to attend networking events and continue meeting people that are in her target market.

Second, she should continue her ad in Relaxation Today. Almost half of her business is coming in from the design as well as offer of her advertisement. Nancy should continue using this venue as a way to promote her business.

Third, even though only five people said they met Nancy Jones at the Chamber, another 25 people wanted to work with her because of a relationship with her. Whether she continues to network at the Chamber or find another venue, she should continue networking and building relationships to grow her business.

Fourth, only two people said her prices were too high. If no one complains about your prices, your business is probably not high enough. This indicates that Nancy Jones fees are near the sweet spot for her ideal clients.

Based on her ideal clients desires for finding a massage therapist, the best way for her to keep and build on her existing client base, is to continue offering great service and establishing relationships with new people.

Also, only five people stated they went to Lavish Touch because of a referral, but almost everyone in the survey said they would go to a massage therapist because of a referral. Nancy needs to promote her referral program to her existing clients in order to increase the number of people that visit her business based on word of mouth referrals.

So, based on a simple survey, Nancy learned which marketing tools are working best, which ones she should expand and which ones should stay the same. This is an easy, low cost way to find out what your customer are thinking. They normally won't talk honestly to you, but you can have a friend, probably for the price of lunch or dinner, do the survey for you.

<u>Sample Marketing Tool Expense Report</u>

Month_____ Year_____

Marketing Tool	Monetary Cost	Amount Distributed	Personal Time Invested	Miles Used On Car	Total Cost	Number of Inquires	Number of Sales or Clients

Follow Up Call Log

Date of Call	Time of Call	Person	Message	Date and Time of Returned Message	Result	Further Follow Up Required

APPENDIX

<u>Marketing Centers/Resources</u>

Small Business Administration – <u>www.SBA.com</u>

SCORE – <u>www.score.org</u>

Small Business Development Centers (SBDC) – check with your local Small Business Administration office to locate the nearest SBDC

Free Management Resource – <u>www.managementhelp.org</u>

American Marketing Association –
<u>www.marketingpower.com</u>

Current statistics sites

U.S. Census Bureau's - <u>www.census.gov</u>

Bureau of Labor and Statistics - <u>http://stats.bls.gov</u>

Federal Government Statistics -
http://www.whitehouse.gov/news/fsbr.html

The Rite Site - www.easidemographics.com

ESRI Business Information Solutions -
www.esribis.com/free_samples/zip_code_searches.htm

Customer service resources

Institute of Customer Service -
http://www.instituteofcustomerservice.com

Customer Service For Dummies by Karen Leland and
Keith Bailey

***Branded Customer Service: The New Competitive
Edge*** by Janelle Barlow and Paul Stewart

Sales resources

Website from *Entrepreneur* that offers free sales tools,
among others, for your business
http://www.entrepreneur.com/sales/index.html

***Selling 101: What Every Successful Sales Professional
Needs to Know*** by Zig Ziglar

*The Ultimate Sales Machine: Turbocharge Your Business with
Relentless Focus on 12 Key Strategies* by Chet Holmes

Selling Sucks: How to Stop Selling and Start Getting Prospects to Buy! by Frank J., Jr. Rumbauskas

Color and design resources

Color: Messages & Meanings by Leatrice Eiseman

Pantone Guide to Communicating with Color by Leatrice Eiseman

Color Graphics: The Power of Color in Design by Karen Triedman and Cheryl Dangel Cullen with Essays by Leatrice Eiseman

United States Patent and Trademark Office - www.uspto.gov

Online Classified Sites

www.craigslist.com

www.webclassifieds.us

www.finditclassifieds.com

www.newfreeclassifieds.com

www.usnewspapers.com/cgi-bin/classifieds/classifieds.cgi

Online Video Sites

www.YouTube.com

www.veoh.com

www.vimeo.com

http://www.metacafe.com/tags/online/

Publishing resources

Writer's Market – www.writersmarket.com – A book as well as online database of more than 6,000 market listings and contact names for periodicals, books, poetry, and contests. Pretty much anything your can write, they have a market for it.

Wooden Horse Publishing – www.woodenhorsepub.com - A news and market resource site for nonfiction periodicals writers.

Public relations resources and media outlets

6 Steps to Free Publicity by Marcia Yudkin

www.newspapers.com

www.sources.com/mnn/MeAindex.htm

www.online-pr.com

www.bizmove.com/media_directory/local-media.htm

www.ecola.com

www.news365.com

www.newslink.org

www.radiotalk.org

www.radio-directory.com

www.tradepub.com

www.newsdirectory.com

www.findarticles.com

News release distribution services (Free)

www.hotproductnews.com

www.industrypages.com

www.prweb.com

Article Submission Sites

www.ezinearticles.com

www.articlesbase.com

www.articlecity.com

Http://internationalpractice.com/business

www.articlecube.com

www.ideasmarketers.com

www.goarticles.com

www.amazines.com

www.articlemarketer.com

www.e-syndicate.net

www.freesticky.com

www.authorconnection.com

www.reprintarcticles.com

www.articlefinders.com

www.articlehub.com

www.free-articles-zone.com

www.article-host.com

Online Phonebook Sites

www.dexknows.com

www.yellowbook.com

www.superpages.com

www.whitepages.com

www.yellowpages.com

www.switchboard.com

ABOUT THE AUTHOR

After self-publishing my first illustrated book in the fourth grade, by using paper covered cardboard and string, I was hooked on writing. At my high school graduation, I predicted I would have my first novel published by the time I was 30. While I don't have my first novel published yet, my nonfiction book, *Open Space Preservation: The History and Practice of the Colorado Front Range* was published in August 2010.

I have owned and operated my own consulting business since 2003. Prior to opening my company, I've worked professionally in the public as well as private sector since 1997. My experience working with the media, making public presentations, facilitating groups, as well as building working relationships all with my sense of humor intact taught me how to be a great listener who creates successful results.

I hold a Bachelor's Degree from Utah State University and a Master's Degree from the University of Colorado in Denver.